Sweet Thoughts

A FRESH APPROACH to the DESSERT COURSE with  CANDEREL®

ROSAMOND RICHARDSON

MARTIN
BOOKS

Published by Martin Books
Simon & Schuster International Group
Fitzwilliam House
32 Trumpington Street
Cambridge CB2 1QY

in association with
Searle Consumer Products
a division of G D Searle & Co Limited
PO Box 53
Lane End Road
High Wycombe
Buckinghamshire HP12 4HL

First published 1989
Text © Rosamond Richardson
Photographs and illustrations,
© Woodhead-Faulkner Ltd 1989

ISBN 0 85941 601 1

NOTES ON RECIPES

All recipes in this book give ingredients in both metric and imperial measures. Use
either set of quantities, but not both, in any one recipe. All teaspoons and tablespoons
are level unless otherwise stated. Egg size is medium (size 3) unless otherwise stated.

Design: Barry Lowenhoff
Colour illustrations: Julia Whatley
Photography: Laurie Evans
Styling: Lesley Richardson
Food preparation for photography: Maxine Clark
Typesetting: Goodfellow & Egan, Cambridge
Printed and bound in Italy by Arnoldo Mondadori Editore

CONTENTS

Pictured on the front cover: Raspberry Mousse (page 34); Apricot Macaroon Ice Cream (page 52); Fresh Fruit Cheesecake (page 92);

Poires à la Bourgignonne (page 86)

Basic Soufflé-omelette with Raspberry Filling (page 125); Scheherazade's Melon (page 110); English Summer Pudding (page 22); Summer-fruits Bombe (page 62)

5

What is Canderel®?

Canderel is a low-calorie sweetener which can be used as an alternative to sugar. It contains the brand sweetener Nutrasweet® which has none of the bitter aftertaste often associated with other sweeteners.

Canderel easily fits into any modern lifestyle and is an ideal sugar substitute for those counting the calories or for those concerned about their health.

Available in tablets and granular form as Canderel Spoonful, Canderel tastes as good as sugar, giving you all the sweetness you need with a fraction of the calories. One tablet contains less than one third of a calorie, and one teaspoon of granular just two calories compared to twenty for one teaspoon of sugar.

For the recipes in this book I have substituted 2 tablespoons of Canderel Spoonful for every 28 g (1 oz) of sugar to give the required sweetness. So, for every 2 tablespoons of Canderel Spoonful you use in preference to sugar, you save over 100 calories!

Canderel is perfect for use in foods where only sweetness is needed – desserts, drinks and toppings as well as for sprinkling on prepared foods, cereals and fruits.

Although Canderel loses its sweetness when exposed to high temperatures for long periods of time, and is therefore not suitable for baking or preserving, it retains its sweetness when stirred into hot sauces or drinks.

Canderel's principal use however is in cold desserts. I have found that it acts not just as a sweetener but also as a flavour enhancer. In particular, it brings out the delicate and distinctive fruit flavours to perfection. Canderel definitely helped me make some of the best desserts I have ever tasted!

Canderel® is a registered trademark of G.D. Searle & Co. Nutrasweet® is a registered trademark of The Nutrasweet Co.

Canderel can help slimming or weight control only as part of a calorie controlled diet.

Eating Desserts The Healthy Way

Eating puddings does not have to be a sin. There are healthy puddings and there are puddings that are obviously not so good for you. But media pressures for fashionable slimness, and a health-education concern over high fat and sugar intake, however laudably motivated, have persuaded many to avoid the dessert course altogether, as a matter of habit. However, such extreme measures need no longer apply; the recipes in this book are an introduction to eating delicious desserts the healthy way.

All the desserts here are low-fat, low-sugar recipes, many of them using fresh fruits. They are sweetened not with sugar but with the low-calorie sweetener Canderel, or with honey. After eating them you will be surprised at how refreshed, full of energy and healthy you feel, instead of heavy and lethargic and rather wishing you hadn't indulged . . .

Like many people I had for years been avoiding eating puddings; I was all too aware of their effect on the waistline and their high fat and sugar content. Nor did I like the way they made me feel – sluggish and fat. Writing this book has brought about a kind of conversion; I started really to enjoy the flavours, so delicately extended and enhanced by the use of Canderel; I felt radiantly healthy afterwards, not disgustingly full. And I actually lost weight while I was testing the recipes and eating them to my heart's content: I have never felt better in my life! The friends I shared them with agreed with me; Canderel has made many converts along the way, by the delightful way it sweetens without masking flavours. All the desserts remain light and fresh; we can now eat them the healthy way.

To keep the fat content down I have used only polyunsaturated margarine – sunflower is my favourite. In some of the recipes I suggest using crème fraîche, because its fat content can be lower than cream. I sometimes use fromage frais, which has a fat content of 40 per cent downwards to the point where it is called fromage blanc, when it may have a fat content of 0 per cent. Low-fat soft cheeses come into their own in some of the recipes, too. Thus the puddings are not as rich as conventional ones. I also avoid using egg yolks, preferring to use just the whites in order to keep the puddings light. And I use skimmed milk instead of full-fat milk.

It is not difficult to be tempted by the alluring display of fresh fruits both native and tropical on our shop shelves and market stalls. I have used them in all their diversity of flavour and colour, relishing the way that the Canderel brings out the very best in them. I also like to use wild fruits where and when possible – blackberries are a great favourite – and I have included recipes using bilberries.

There are desserts for all seasons in this book, desserts for all occasions too, whether family, formal or informal. I have converted recipes from classical cookery sources, famous desserts to suit the modern taste for lightness, freshness and healthy eating. The fruit sauces are delightful with their delicate, fresh, fruity flavours. The range of recipes is mouthwatering: soufflés, mousses and fools are all there; feathery crêpes and spectacular soufflé-omelettes; delicate ices and bombes which are a revelation in taste and freshness. Using fruits from all over the world, I have included fruit salads and compotes as well as crumbles and traditional family puddings. The cheesecakes and syllabubs are all low fat, and delectable, and there are recipes for stuffed-fruit desserts. Where the puddings need baking, I have used clear honey, as Canderel loses its sweetness on baking. Over this whole range of recipes the results are refreshingly light and delicately flavoured, wonderfully sweet without being cloying or heavy. Healthy desserts are here to stay.

Rosamond Richardson

There are few things more enjoyable throughout the year than choosing fruits to make into a delicious dessert, and in this book I give you a wide choice, whether they are native favourites such as apples and pears, or tropical delicacies, like mangoes, pineapples and guavas. With Canderel it is possible to enjoy fruit, so nutritious and healthy, without lashings of sugar. I find that Canderel actually enhances the flavours of fruits and does not mask the taste as other sweeteners often do. Fruit is undoubtedly good for you: high in vitamins and minerals, and fibrous, too (especially bananas, blackberries and plums). A light, fruity dessert is not only a delectable way to finish a meal, it is also a contribution to your balanced diet.

The fruits in this book fall into five main categories: pip fruits (apples and pears), stone fruits (such as plums and peaches), soft fruits and berries (anything from rhubarb, to blackberries and the currants), citrus fruits and exotic fruit (from the familiar banana to the mango and guava).

Most fruits complement each other well, but some form particularly happy pairs, for example, apricots and kiwi-fruit, peaches and strawberries, pears and grapes, raspberries and strawberries, bananas and pineapples, blackberries and bananas, blackberries and apples, peaches and oranges, apricots and oranges. You'll find a recipe for all seasons here, to suit your particular taste, your mood and the time of year.

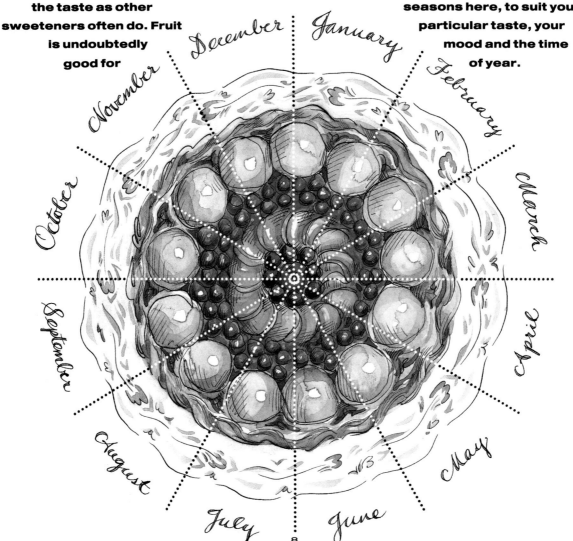

December   January

November   February

October   March

September   April

August   May

July   June

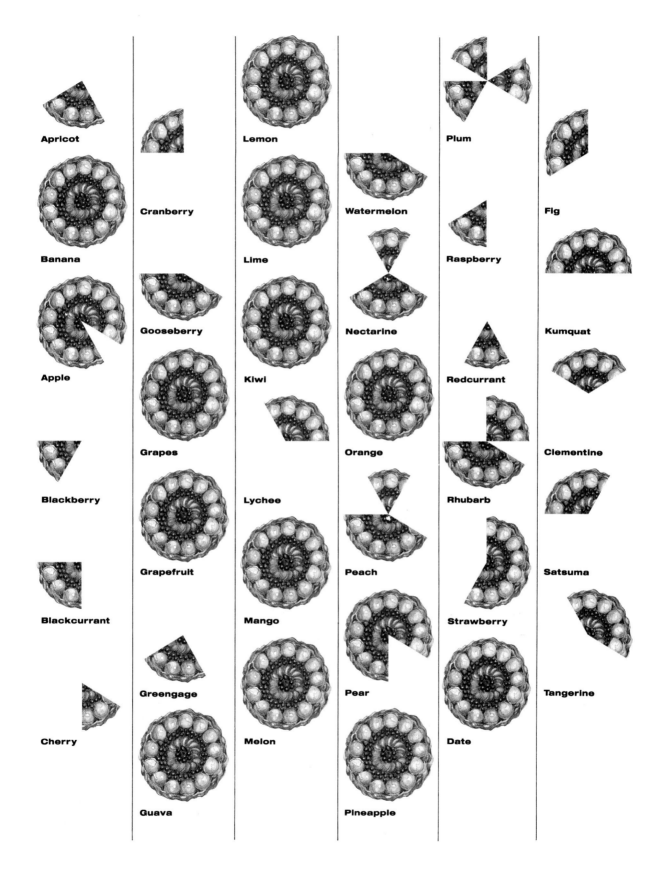

Apricot

Banana

Apple

Blackberry

Blackcurrant

Cherry

Cranberry

Gooseberry

Grapes

Grapefruit

Greengage

Guava

Lemon

Lime

Kiwi

Lychee

Mango

Melon

Watermelon

Nectarine

Orange

Peach

Pear

Pineapple

Plum

Raspberry

Redcurrant

Rhubarb

Strawberry

Date

Fig

Kumquat

Clementine

Satsuma

Tangerine

CLASSIC DESSERTS
THE
MODERN WAY

POIRES BELLE HÉLÈNE

SERVES 6

This famous French dessert consists of pears poached in a vanilla syrup, chilled, then arranged with a scoop of vanilla ice cream and coated with chocolate sauce. It has proved to be irresistible over the years.

Place the pears in a large ovenproof dish. Combine the honey with the lemon juice, water, and vanilla pod, and stir over a low heat until the mixture boils. Remove from the

6 large, ripe pears, peeled, cored and halved

6 tbs clear honey

4 tbs lemon juice

450 ml (¾ pint) water

1 10 cm (4-inch) vanilla pod

6 scoops Basic Ice Cream (see page 50)

450 ml (¾ pint) Chocolate Sauce (see page 120)

4 tbs slivered almonds, toasted

Heat the oven to Gas Mark 3/ 160°C/325°F.

heat, pour over the pears and cook in the oven until the pears are tender, about 10 minutes, basting from time to time. Remove from the oven and leave to cool in the syrup. Remove the vanilla pod and chill.

For each serving, arrange two pear halves in a glass dish, place a scoop of ice cream in the centre, coat with Chocolate Sauce and sprinkle with toasted almonds.

FRENCH APPLE FLAN

SERVES 6

A well-made apple tart is one of the joys of French confectionery; a light pastry base is topped with Crème Patissière and covered with lightly grilled slices of dessert apple. Finally the tart is glazed – usually with apricot jam, but here I have made a glaze with honey.

Line a 30 cm (12-inch) flan tin with the pastry, and bake blind (see page 124). Cool on a rack. Spread the pastry case with the Crème Patissière.

Sweet Crust Pastry, using 275 g (9 oz) flour (see page 124)

Crème Patissière (see page 115)

750 g (1½ lb) dessert apples, preferably Coxes, peeled, cored and sliced thinly

40 g (1½ oz) sunflower margarine

4 tbs clear honey

2 tbs water

Heat the oven to Gas Mark 3/ 160°C/325°F.

Melt the margarine. Arrange the apple slices on a baking tray and brush them with the margarine.

Place under a medium grill and cook until slightly softened and golden on top. Cool, then place in overlapping concentric circles on top of the Crème Patissière.

Heat the honey with the water in a small saucepan and stir until blended. Then boil until it thickens, about 3–4 minutes, and cool for 1–2 minutes before brushing over the apple slices. Chill the flan until ready to serve. Lovely with crème fraîche or Greek yogurt.

APPLE CHARLOTTE

SERVES 6–8

Family food. I love to make this dessert in the autumn when Bramley apples are abundant – they are to my mind the very best of cooking apples and make delicious puddings. My children love this charlotte – it is tasty, satisfying and a perfect finish to a weekend meal.

Butter an 18 cm (7-inch) loose-bottomed cake tin.

Trim the crusts from the bread. Using about half the margarine, spread the bread on one side only and cut two-thirds of the slices into 3 equal strips per slice. Line the sides of the tin with these, buttered side out. Cut the remaining

---

10–12 thin slices wholemeal bread

---

175 g (6 oz) sunflower margarine

1.25 kg (2½ lb) cooking apples (preferably Bramleys), peeled, cored and sliced

---

grated peel of 2 lemons

½ tsp freshly grated nutmeg

½ tsp ground ginger

---

6 tbs clear honey, warmed

Heat the oven to Gas Mark 5/ 190°C/375°F

---

slices into triangles and use half of these to line the bottom of the tin so that the edges fit neatly.

Put the prepared apples into a dish with a little water, cover and bake in the oven for 12–15 minutes until tender but not mushy. Add the

lemon peel, the rest of the margarine, the spices and the honey. Mix until well blended. Spoon into the bread-lined tin. Cover the top with the rest of the bread triangles, trim the tops, place the tin on a baking sheet and return to the oven for 30 minutes.

Allow to stand for at least 10 minutes before sliding a knife between the inside of the tin and the bread slices. Then place a serving plate over the top, invert it sharply, and lift the tin off.

Serve hot or chilled. Either way, it is delicious with Greek yogurt.

CHERRY CLAFOUTIS

SERVES 4

The French invented this homely pudding, which is a kind of fruit pastry or thick pancake. You can make it with apples or pears or plums, but I find that cherries make a particularly good clafoutis.

Butter a 30 cm (12-inch) shallow pie dish. Mix the breadcrumbs with the cardamom or cinnamon, and sprinkle

---

3 tbs fine dry wholemeal breadcrumbs

½ tsp ground cardamom or cinnamon

---

500 g (1 lb) fresh cherries, stoned and halved

---

3 eggs

---

75 g (3 oz) plain flour

---

450 ml (¾ pint) skimmed milk

---

4 tbs clear honey, heated gently

Heat the oven to Gas Mark 4/ 180°C/350°F.

---

over the bottom of the dish. Spread the fruit over the breadcrumbs.

Beat the eggs thoroughly, then add the flour and mix well. Stir in the milk and beat again, then beat in the honey. Pour the mixture over the cherries and bake in the oven for 45 minutes, until set and golden. Allow to cool a little – it will sink – then serve warm with crème fraîche.

Apple Charlotte (page 12); Cherry Clafoutis (page 12)

BILBERRY PIE
SERVES 6—8

The first time I tasted bilberries was in Scandinavia, and ever since then I have sought them out at home. They are luscious on the palate and delightful to look at – dusky blue with a bloom on the skins.

Line a 25 cm (10-inch) pie dish with two-thirds of the pastry rolled out thinly. Melt the honey with the water and lemon juice over a gentle heat until well amalgamated, and

Sweet Crust Pastry, using 350 g (12 oz) flour (see page 124)
6 tbs clear honey
1 tbs water
1 tbs lemon juice
1 kg (2 lb) bilberries, topped and tailed
1 egg, beaten
Heat the oven to Gas Mark 4/ 180°C/350°F.

mix into the prepared bilberries. Stir well, then put the fruit onto the pastry shell.

Cut the remaining rolled-out pastry into a round slightly larger than the pie dish and lay it over the top. Seal the edges with water and press down with a fork. Brush with the beaten egg. Cut a small hole in the centre to allow the steam to escape. Put onto a preheated baking sheet, and bake in the oven for 20–25 minutes until the pastry is golden brown. Serve hot or warm, with Crème Anglaise (see page 120) or crème fraîche.

PEAR TATIN
SERVES 4—6

A tarte Tatin – or, more properly, a tarte des Demoiselles Tatin – is a kind of upside-down fruit pie. Despite this banal description, a Tatin is superb and the Demoiselles Tatin have given their name to a culinary classic.

Grease a pie dish about 20 cm (8-inches) in diameter and 5 cm (2-inches) deep.

In a small saucepan melt the margarine and honey with the lemon peel and cinnamon. Stir over a low

25 g (1 oz) sunflower margarine
6 tbs clear honey
1 tsp grated lemon peel
½ tsp ground cinnamon
1.25 kg (2½ lb) ripe pears, peeled, cored and sliced
250 g (8 oz) Sweet Crust Pastry (see page 124)
Heat the oven to Gas Mark 6/ 200°C/400°F.

heat until blended, and set aside.

Arrange the pears in layers in a circular pattern over the bottom of the dish, pouring the honey mixture over each layer as you go. Roll out the pastry and cut into a circle slightly larger than the pie dish. Place over the pears and tuck the edges of the pastry inside the dish. Cut a small hole in the centre to allow steam to escape. Bake for about 40 minutes on a low shelf in the oven, covering the crust with foil after 25 minutes. Cool on a rack in the dish and then chill thoroughly.

When ready to serve, slide a knife around the edge of the tart, put a serving plate on top and invert it on to the plate. Eat it on the same day, served with crème fraîche.

Pear Tatin (page 14); French Apple Flan (page 11); Bilberry Pie (page 14)

Poires Belle Hélène (page 11); Mille-feuilles (page 18); Exotic Fruit Tart (page 19); Marrons Mont Blanc (page 19)

MILLE-FEUILLES
SERVES 4

A wonderful dessert for a summer party, this is also much loved by children. So when fresh strawberries are in season I make mille-feuilles quite frequently for family and friends alike. It is very simple to prepare, yet looks rewardingly spectacular. This can also be made 'out of season', using the same quantity of a mixture of grapes and bananas.

Roll out the pastry into a large rectangle 40 × 33 cm (16 × 13 inches) and about 25 mm (¼ inch) thick. Trim the edges. Mark into 4 down the long sides, and cut into equal pieces, each 12.5 × 30 cm

---

350 g (12 oz) frozen puff pastry, thawed

---

4 tbs Canderel Spoonful

---

350 g (12 oz) strawberries, hulled and sliced thinly, plus a few extra to decorate

---

250 g (8 oz) crème fraîche

---

2 egg whites, beaten stiffly

Heat the oven to Gas Mark 7/ 220°C/425°F.

(4 × 12 inches). Prick the surfaces, and place on a well-greased baking sheet. Bake in the oven for 12 minutes until well risen and golden. Cool on a rack, then cut in half lengthways, to make 8 pieces.

Sprinkle 2 tablespoons of the Canderel Spoonful over the sliced strawberries, mix well and leave to

stand for 10 minutes.

Mix the crème fraîche with a fork and sweeten with the rest of the Canderel Spoonful. Fold in the stiffly beaten egg whites.

To assemble, slice each piece of pastry in half across the middle and sandwich the layers with the whipped cream and strawberries, leaving enough of the crème fraîche mixture to decorate the top of each one with a little mound. Finally, cut the reserved strawberries in half and place a half, cut side down, in the centre of each mound. Serve on a flat plate or board as soon as possible after assembly.

PEACH MELBA
SERVES 6

This most famous of desserts was created in honour of the renowned opera-singer, Dame Nellie Melba. The raspberry sauce is not cooked – the fresh fruits are blended in a liquidiser and passed through a sieve, and sweetened to taste. Peaches and ice cream make up the rest of this exquisite concoction.

Put the peaches into a bowl and pour

---

6 large ripe peaches

---

250 g (8 oz) crème fraîche

---

2 tsp vanilla essence

---

1 egg white

---

6 scoops Basic Ice Cream (see page 50)

Melba Sauce (see page 122)

---

50 g (2 oz) slivered almonds, toasted

---

boiling water over them. Leave for 1 minute, then drain and peel them. Cut in half and remove the stones.

Mix the crème fraîche with the remaining Canderel Spoonful and the vanilla essence, beat the egg white stiffly and fold in.

To assemble, put a scoop of ice cream into the bottom of each individual glass, place 2 peach halves on top and coat with the Melba Sauce. Top with the crème fraîche mixture, then scatter over the toasted almonds. Serve immediately.

MARRONS MONT BLANC

SERVES 8

This French dessert is meant to represent a great mountain topped with snow. This is achieved by making a ring of light chestnut purée, and filling it with a pile of fluffy, white crème Chantilly.

Liquidise the chestnut purée with 6 tablespoons of the Canderel Spoonful and the milk to bring it to the consistency of thick cream. Flavour with the vanilla essence.

Slice the trifle sponge cakes in half lengthways. Puncture their

350 g (12 oz) can of unsweetened chestnut purée
8 tbs Canderel Spoonful
150 ml (¼ pint) skimmed milk
2 tsp vanilla essence
4 trifle sponge cakes
150 ml (¼ pint) black coffee
1 tbs kirsch (optional)
500 g (1 lb) crème fraîche
1 egg white, beaten stiffly
plain chocolate, grated, to decorate

surfaces, and lay them on a large, round serving plate. Sprinkle with the black coffee, flavoured with the

kirsch if desired. Press the chestnut purée through a sieve, or a potato-ricer if you have one, to make a bank or nest shape around the edge of the sponges (the purée emerges looking like vermicelli).

Mash the remaining Canderel Spoonful into the crème fraîche and fold the stiffly beaten egg white into this crème Chantilly. Pile into the centre of the chestnut nest to make a dome shape, and sprinkle the top with grated chocolate. Chill before serving.

EXOTIC FRUIT TART

SERVES 8

This lovely tart, fresh and light, is a pretty sight with all its soft fruit colours. Instead of the traditional crème patissière, the base is made with fromage frais and curd cheese flavoured with orange juice: a perfect vehicle for a selection of fresh exotic fruits.

Sweet Crust Pastry, using 175 g (6 oz) flour (see page 124)
125 g (4 oz) fromage frais
2 tbs fresh orange juice
2 tbs Canderel Spoonful
50 g (2 oz) curd cheese
500 g (1 lb) mixed fruits (nectarines, kiwifruits, mangoes, starfruits, seedless grapes, orange segments, slices of banana dipped in lemon juice, strawberries), prepared and sliced
Heat the oven to Gas Mark 3/ 160°C/325°F.

Line a 20 cm (8-inch) flan tin with the pastry and bake blind (see page 124). Cool on a rack.

Mix together the fromage frais, orange juice, Canderel Spoonful and curd cheese and beat until smooth. Spoon into the cold pastry case and smooth down with a knife. Arrange the sliced fruits decoratively over the top, and chill.

PARIS-BREST AUX FRAISES

SERVES 6—8

This spectacular ring of choux pastry is filled with fresh strawberries and decorated with crème Chantilly. It is wonderful as a midsummer dessert and, although the preparation takes some time, it is well worth it. Eat it on the day that you make it, because it becomes soggy if left overnight.

Put the milk and margarine into a small, heavy saucepan and bring slowly to boiling point, so that the margarine melts by the time the milk boils. Add the flour and beat until the sides of the pan are clean. Cool slightly, then add the eggs singly, beating until each one is thoroughly blended. Cool a little, and stir in the warmed honey. Cover and chill.

Spoon or pipe on to a greased baking sheet in a large ring about 30 cm (12 inches) in diameter.

FOR THE CHOUX PASTRY:

300 ml (½ pint) skimmed milk

125 g (4 oz) sunflower margarine

150 g (5 oz) plain flour, sifted

4 eggs

2 tbs clear honey, warmed

2 tbs flaked almonds

FOR THE FILLING:

750 g (1½ lb) strawberries, hulled and sliced

6 tbs Canderel Spoonful

2 tsp vanilla essence

250 g (8 oz) crème fraîche

2 egg whites

TO DECORATE:

8 strawberries hulled and halved

4 mint sprigs

Heat the oven to Gas Mark 7/ 220°C/425°F.

Sprinkle the top with the flaked almonds. Bake in the oven for 20 minutes, then turn the heat down to Gas Mark 3/160°C/325°F and continue baking for a further 20 minutes. Cover the top with foil for the last 15 minutes so that it does not brown too deeply. Cool on a rack for a few minutes, then cut in half around the length of the ring, and set the lid to one side. Leave to cool completely.

Put the sliced strawberries into a bowl and mix with 3 tablespoons of the Canderel Spoonful. Flavour with the vanilla essence. Mix the remaining Canderel Spoonful into the crème fraîche, beat the egg whites stiffly and fold in.

Pack the base of the choux pastry ring with the strawberries and spread half of the crème Chantilly over them. Cover with the lid, and pipe the rest of the crème Chantilly over the top. Decorate with the halved strawberries and sprigs of mint, and serve as soon as possible.

Paris-brest aux Fraises (page 20)

RIZ À L'IMPÉRATRICE

SERVES 10

A French classic, this deliciously creamy rice pudding is irresistible. You can also make it with dried peaches or apricots if you prefer these to glacé fruits, or even try it with fresh soft fruits in season.

Mix the glacé fruits with the kirsch and set aside. Cook the rice for 5 minutes in a large pan of boiling water. Drain thoroughly. Bring the milk and margarine to the boil in a large flameproof casserole. Stir in the rice, the honey and vanilla

125 g (4 oz) mixed glacé fruits, chopped finely
4 tbs kirsch
125 g (4 oz) long-grain white rice
450 ml (¾ pint) skimmed milk
25 g (1 oz) sunflower margarine
2–3 tbs clear honey
1 tsp vanilla essence
450 ml (¾ pint) Crème Anglaise (see page 120)
4 tbs Canderel Spoonful
250 g (8 oz) crème fraîche or fromage frais
glacé fruits, to decorate
Heat the oven to Gas Mark 2/ 150°C/300°F.

essence and bring to simmering point. Put into the oven and cook for about 40 minutes, until the milk is absorbed and the rice tender.

Make the Crème Anglaise and stir in the glacé fruits while it is still hot. Stir the rice into this custard. Allow to cool a little, then add the Canderel Spoonful. Stir thoroughly and chill. Just before it sets, beat in the crème fraîche or fromage frais. Chill overnight, and serve decorated with more glacé fruits.

ENGLISH SUMMER PUDDING

SERVES 6

Summer pudding is one of England's great classics. One of the advantages of this dessert is that it requires almost no cooking – perfect food for hot weather.

Place all the prepared fruits in a large pan with the water. Stir over a gentle heat until well mixed, then simmer gently for about 5 minutes. Cool. Add the Canderel Spoonful and stir in thoroughly.

250 g (8 oz) redcurrants or blackcurrants, topped and tailed
350 g (12 oz) cherries, stoned and halved
250 g (8 oz) raspberries, hulled
5 tbs water
6 tbs Canderel Spoonful
10–12 thin slices white or wholemeal bread

Butter an 18 cm (7-inch) cake tin or pudding basin. Trim the crusts from the bread. Cut some of the slices in half lengthways and line

the sides of the tin. Cut more of the slices into triangles and line the bottom of the tin, making sure that the edges fit neatly. Fill with the fruit and enough of the juices to moisten the bread. Cover the top with additional bread triangles. Place a flat plate on the pudding, weight it down and chill overnight.

To serve, invert on to a serving dish and pass a bowl of crème fraîche around with it.

LIGHT SOUFFLÉS, MOUSSES AND FOOLS

TO PREPARE A SOUFFLÉ DISH

Grease a 12.5 cm (5-inch) diameter soufflé dish. Wrap a length of foil or waxed paper around the outside of the dish so that it stands 5–7.5 cm (2–3 inches) above the rim. Fasten securely with string.

When the soufflé or mousse is ready to serve, unfasten the paper very carefully before giving the dessert its final decorative touches.

DECORATING MOUSSES AND COLD SOUFFLÉS

This is very much a matter of individual taste. You can pipe whipped cream around the edge and on top of the dessert, or simply sprinkle finely grated chocolate over the top. Leaves from the fruit that you are using look really pretty on the plate around the dessert, or in a pattern on top. In summer you can decorate your desserts with flowers, or use extra fruit sliced decoratively and arranged prettily on and around the pudding.

RHUBARB FOOL
SERVES 6

Rhubarb is the first of our garden fruits to ripen, and has traditionally been an ingredient in English foods for many years. In early cookbooks the recipes show that a fool was enriched with eggs and cream, but here a simple Crème Anglaise and Greek yogurt make for a healthier and more summery dessert.

750 g (1½ lb) rhubarb
5–6 tbs Canderel Spoonful
Crème Anglaise (see page 120)
125 g (4 oz) Greek yogurt

Wash and trim the rhubarb and cut the stems into 2.5 cm (1-inch) lengths. Place in a saucepan with a little water, cover and simmer until the fruit is very soft – about 10–12 minutes. Allow to cool, then sweeten to taste with the Canderel Spoonful.

Stir the Crème Anglaise into the fruit. Blend in a liquidiser with the yogurt. Check for sweetness and add more Canderel Spoonful if necessary. Chill. Serve in a bowl or individual glasses.

MANGO FOOL
SERVES 4

The best place to eat mangoes, so the Indians say, is in the bath: it is a messy business. But, for a more formal event, try this summery, delicate fool.

Purée the prepared mangoes with the Crème Anglaise in a liquidiser.

2 large ripe mangoes, peeled and stoned
Crème Anglaise (see page 120)
2 tsp lemon juice
175 g (6 oz) crème fraîche or Greek yogurt
2–3 tbs Canderel Spoonful

Stir in the lemon juice. Mix the crème fraîche or Greek yogurt with the Canderel Spoonful and stir it into the fruit custard until well blended. Check the flavour, and add more Canderel Spoonful if necessary. Chill thoroughly before serving in a bowl or individual glasses.

TANGERINE MOUSSE

SERVES 6

Prepare the soufflé dish (see page 24). Soak the gelatine in the lemon juice. Beat the egg yolks, add the Canderel Spoonful and beat again until pale and thick. Grate the peel of the tangerines finely and stir into the egg-yolk mixture. Peel the fruit and chop it finely, reserving the juices. Add the warmed milk gradually to the egg mixture, stirring well. Whisk over a pan of hot water until the mixture is thick enough to coat the back of a spoon, being

margarine for greasing
15 g (½ oz) gelatine
2 tbs lemon juice
3 eggs, separated
4 tbs Canderel Spoonful
4 tangerines
150 ml (¼ pint) milk, warmed
4–5 tbs crème fraîche or fromage frais
4 tangerines, segmented, to decorate
Heat the oven to Gas Mark 5/ 190°C/375°F.

careful not to let it boil.

Put the gelatine and lemon

juice into a small saucepan and heat gently until the gelatine is dissolved. Add it to the egg mixture with the finely chopped tangerine and its juices. Stir over a bowl full of ice until it begins to set. Fold in the crème fraîche or fromage frais. Then beat the egg whites to stiff peaks and fold into the fruit mixture. Spoon into the soufflé dish and chill til set.

Decorate, just before serving, with concentric circles of tangerine segments.

LIGHT CHOCOLATE SOUFFLÉ

SERVES 6

This soufflé is made with cocoa and black coffee, both strong and pungent flavours – yet the dish is light and not too rich. The mixture separates into a scrumptious thick custard with a light fluffy topping to make a delicious finish to a meal.

Soak the gelatine in the coffee. Prepare a 12.5 cm (5-inch) soufflé dish (see page 24). Put the milk and the cocoa powder into a pan and bring slowly to the boil, then simmer

15 g (½ oz) gelatine
2 tbs strong black coffee
margarine for greasing
450 ml (¾ pint) skimmed milk
25 g (1 oz) cocoa powder
3 eggs, separated
4 tbs Canderel Spoonful
2–3 tbs crème fraîche or double or whipping cream, whipped

for 1 minute, stirring well. Beat the egg yolks until they are light, then pour on the flavoured milk. Mix well and return to the pan. Stir, without

allowing to boil, until the mixture thickens. Strain into a bowl, cool, and stir in the Canderel Spoonful. Dissolve the soaked gelatine in the coffee over a low heat and add .

Set the bowl on a large bowl of ice and chill in the fridge until nearly set, stirring from time to time. Remove from the ice and quickly fold in the crème fraîche or cream. Whisk the egg whites until they are stiff peaks, and fold them in. Turn at once into the soufflé dish, and leave.

Tangerine Mousse (page 26); Light Chocolate Soufflé (page 26)

W H I T E   C H O C O L A T E   M O U S S E
S E R V E S   4 – 6

The combination of white chocolate with black coffee is simply stunning. This mousse makes a dessert course with a difference, irresistibly creamy in texture and with flavours that linger on the palate.

Soak the gelatine in the black coffee. Melt the white chocolate in a bowl over hot water (it will be quite stiff but will thin out in the next process). Cream the margarine with the

15 g (½ oz) gelatine
3 tbs black coffee
175 g (6 oz) white chocolate
40 g (1½ oz) sunflower margarine
2 tbs Canderel Spoonful
4 eggs, separated
125 g (4 oz) crème fraîche or Greek yogurt

Canderel Spoonful and gradually add the lukewarm chocolate.

In a separate bowl, beat the egg yolks until they are pale, then fold them into the margarine and white-chocolate mixture. Heat the gelatine and coffee gently in a small saucepan, and stir until the gelatine is dissolved, then add carefully to the mixture. Fold in the crème fraîche or Greek yogurt.

Beat the egg whites until they form stiff peaks, then fold in quickly and evenly. Pour into a bowl or into individual glasses, and serve chilled.

N E C T A R I N E   A N D   M A N G O   S O U F F L É
S E R V E S   6

This exquisite chilled soufflé is a delicate, light, memorable dessert. In spring or summer decorate it with a feathery sprig of fennel or a nasturtium flower or two.

Soak the gelatine in the water. Prepare a soufflé dish (see page 24). Whisk the egg yolks with 4 tablespoons of the Canderel Spoonful until thick, light and

15 g (½ oz) gelatine
3 tbs water
margarine for greasing
3 eggs, separated
6 tbs Canderel Spoonful
250 g (8 oz) Greek yogurt
250 g (8 oz) peeled and stoned nectarines, sliced
250 g (8 oz) peeled and stoned mango, chopped
2 tsp lemon juice

creamy, and stir in the yogurt. Add the prepared fruit to the mixture with the rest of the Canderel Spoonful and the lemon juice. Blend in a liquidiser to a rough purée.

Heat the soaked gelatine very gently in a small saucepan, until it is completely dissolved. Fold quickly into the purée. Finally, whisk the egg whites until they are very stiff, and fold them in lightly but thoroughly. Pour into the soufflé dish and chill until set.

KIWI FOOL
SERVES 4–6

A kiwi fool is subtlety itself, both in colour and flavour. The palest of greens speckled with tiny black seeds, it makes a pretty and deliciously light dessert for a summery meal al fresco.

750 g (1½ lb) very ripe kiwifruit, peeled
300 ml (½ pint) Crème Anglaise (see page 120)
4–6 tbs Canderel Spoonful
250 g (8 oz) crème fraîche or Greek yogurt

Purée the kiwifruit with the Crème Anglaise. Mix the Canderel Spoonful into the crème fraîche or Greek yogurt and stir into the custard mixture. Blend thoroughly, and chill.

BLACKCURRANT MOUSSE
SERVES 4

In high summer, when the blackcurrant crop is ripe and boxes of the glistening berries cram the grocers' fruit shelves, I love to make this delectable mousse. Light and fluffy, fresh and fruity, it is really sensational.

Soak the gelatine in the cold water. Prepare a 12.5 cm (5-inch) soufflé dish (see page 24). Put the

15 g (½ oz) gelatine
150 ml (¼ pint) water
margarine for greasing
350 g (12 oz) fresh blackcurrants, topped and tailed
4 tbs Canderel Spoonful
175 g (6 oz) crème fraîche or double or whipping cream, whipped
3 egg whites

blackcurrants in a liquidiser and blend them to a purée. Stir in the

Canderel Spoonful.

Heat the soaked gelatine gently in a small saucepan until completely dissolved, then quickly add to the fruit purée. When evenly mixed, fold in the crème fraîche or cream. Chill until it begins to set, then fold in the very stiffly beaten egg whites. Spoon into the soufflé dish and chill for 8 hours or overnight, until completely set.

White Chocolate Mousse (page 28); Nectarine and Mango Soufflé (page 28); Kiwi Fool (page 29); Light Strawberry Mousse (page 36)

CHOCOLATE AND ORANGE MOUSSE
SERVES 6

The classic combination of chocolate and orange is particularly delicious when its richness is lightened by the use of yogurt, as in this recipe.

Soak the gelatine in the orange juice. Beat the egg yolks and mix with the melted chocolate and the finely grated orange peel. Stir in the yogurt. Heat the soaked gelatine gently over a low heat until completely dissolved, then add to the mixture carefully.

Whisk the egg whites until stiff and beat in the Canderel Spoonful. Fold lightly but thoroughly into the chocolate mixture. Spoon into a pretty glass bowl or individual dishes, and chill for 6 hours or overnight until set.

15 g (½ oz) gelatine
grated peel and juice of 1 small orange
4 eggs, separated
250 g (8 oz) plain chocolate, melted
250 g (8 oz) natural set yogurt
4 tbs Canderel Spoonful
a sprig of mint, to decorate

SOUFFLÉ EXOTIQUE
SERVES 6

This is a hot soufflé made with tropical fruits. Here I use pineapple and banana, but you can also make it with mango and kiwifruit, or with nectarines and grapes. It is quite a party piece.

Prepare a 12.5 cm (5-inch) soufflé dish (see page 24). Beat the egg yolks with the honey and, when the mixture is thick and creamy, fold in the flour. Pour the heated milk slowly over the mixture, return to the pan and heat gently until it thickens, stirring all the time.

Slice the bananas finely and chop the pineapple. Add both to the custard base. Allow to cool a little. Beat the egg whites stiffly and fold delicately into the mixture. Pour into a greased soufflé dish and bake in the oven for 20–25 minutes.

Serve as soon as the soufflé is fully risen and a knife inserted in the centre comes out almost clean.

margarine for greasing
4 eggs, separated
3 tbs clear honey, warmed
50 g (2 oz) plain flour, sifted
300 ml (½ pint) skimmed milk, heated
2 bananas, peeled
250 g (8 oz) fresh pineapple, peeled and cored
Heat the oven to Gas Mark 5/ 190°C/375°F.

Soufflé Exotique (page 32); Blackcurrant Mousse (page 29); Chocolate and Orange Mousse (page 32)

COFFEE MOUSSE
SERVES 6–8

The creaminess of Greek yogurt gives this mousse a smooth texture, while its dark and distinctive flavour makes it the perfect end to a meal.

Soak the gelatine in the water. Beat the egg yolks in a bowl. Bring the milk to the boil and pour on to the yolks, whisking well. Return the mixture to the saucepan. Reheat the custard until it thickens enough to coat the back of a spoon, being

20 g (¾ oz) gelatine
5 tbs hot water
4 eggs, separated
600 ml (1 pint) skimmed milk
2 tbs black coffee, made with 3 tsp instant coffee
2–3 tbs Canderel Spoonful
450 ml (¾ pint) Greek yogurt
plain chocolate, grated, to decorate

careful not to allow it to boil. Leave it to cool.

Heat the soaked gelatine gently in a small saucepan until it is runny, then stir into the custard with the coffee and Canderel Spoonful.

When the mixture is cold, fold in the Greek yogurt. Whisk the egg whites until stiff and then fold into the mixture carefully. Pour into a glass bowl or individual dishes and chill until set. Decorate the top with grated plain chocolate.

RASPBERRY MOUSSE
SERVES 8

A perfect dessert for midsummer, when fresh raspberries are abundant, this mousse has a smooth, creamy texture and is lightness itself.

Toss the raspberries with 2 tablespoons of the Canderel Spoonful and set aside for 10 minutes. Soak the gelatine in the water. Prepare a soufflé dish (see page 24). Liquidise the raspberries, then pass them through a sieve.

Beat the egg yolks with the rest of the Canderel Spoonful until light and creamy, then fold in the

350 g (12 oz) raspberries, hulled
5 tbs Canderel Spoonful
15 g (½ oz) gelatine
4 tbs water
margarine for greasing
4 eggs, separated
grated peel of 1 lemon
2 tbs lemon juice
175 g (6 oz) crème fraîche or double or whipping cream, whipped
TO DECORATE:
8 raspberries
a sprig of mint

lemon peel. In a small saucepan mix

the soaked gelatine with the lemon juice and stir over a low heat until the gelatine has dissolved. Cool a little before folding into the egg-yolk mixture. Then fold in the crème fraîche or cream. Stir in the raspberry purée. Beat the egg whites until very stiff, and fold them in evenly and quickly. Pour into the soufflé dish and chill for several hours until set.

Arrange the whole raspberries around the edge just before serving, and place a sprig of mint on the centre.

Chilled Lemon Soufflé (page 36); Raspberry Mousse (page 34); Coffee Mousse (page 34)

CHILLED LEMON SOUFFLÉ
SERVES 6

Refreshingly tart, this lemon soufflé is food for all seasons. I often use this recipe when I have a buffet party, and it is also excellent after a summer salad.

Soak the gelatine in the lemon juice. Prepare a 12.5 cm (5-inch) soufflé dish (see page 24). Beat the egg yolks with the Canderel Spoonful until pale and thick. Add the lemon

2 tbs gelatine
finely grated peel and juice of 3 lemons
margarine for greasing
6 eggs, separated
6 tbs Canderel Spoonful
300 g (10 oz) crème fraîche or fromage frais
strips of lemon peel, to decorate

peel.

Put the soaked gelatine into a small saucepan and stir over a low heat until dissolved. Fold quickly and evenly into the egg-yolk mixture, then fold in the crème fraîche or fromage frais. Beat the egg whites until very stiff, and fold evenly into the mixture. Put into the soufflé dish and chill until set. Just before serving, decorate with curls of lemon peel.

LIGHT STRAWBERRY MOUSSE
SERVES 4

Light and summery, this dessert is a long-standing favourite of mine. It is incredibly simple to make, and retains the delicate and distinctive flavour of fresh strawberries. The palest of soft pinks, the mousse looks lovely decorated with a few rose petals scattered over the top.

350 g (12 oz) strawberries, hulled
3 tbs Canderel Spoonful
250 g (8 oz) crème fraîche or fromage frais
1 egg white

Put the strawberries in a liquidiser. Blend to a purée, then press through a sieve to remove the pips. Stir in the Canderel Spoonful. Fold in the crème fraîche or fromage frais and blend thoroughly, then beat the egg white stiffly and fold in.

Spoon into a decorative bowl or individual dishes and chill thoroughly before serving.

FEATHERY CRÊPES AND SOUFFLÉ OMELETTES

CRÊPES FITZGERALD

SERVES 6

A sophisticated idea, which is said to have been named after the author F. Scott Fitzgerald, this makes a really unusual party piece.

Melt the margarine in a heavy-bottomed saucepan. When it has become quite hot, sauté the sliced strawberries quickly. Pour the liqueur into the pan, set a match to it

40 g (1½ oz) sunflower margarine
350 g (12 oz) strawberries, hulled and sliced
3 tbs Grand Marnier or brandy
250 g (8 oz) curd cheese or fromage frais
4 tbs crème fraîche or Greek yogurt
2–3 tbs Canderel Spoonful, plus a little extra for sprinkling
12 Basic Crêpes (see page 125)
borage flowers, to decorate

and flambé the fruit. Put into a bowl and cool a little. Mix the curd cheese and crème fraîche with the Canderel Spoonful, stir in the strawberries, and chill.

Place some of the mixture along the middle of each crêpe, roll them up and sprinkle with Canderel Spoonful just before serving. Decorate with a few borage flowers.

Crêpes Fitzgerald (page 38)

Gâteau de Crêpes (page 43); Crêpes Suzette with Nectarines (page 42); Crêpes au Moka (page 43);

Gingered Peach Soufflé-omelette (page 42)

CRÊPES SUZETTE WITH NECTARINES

SERVES 6

Crêpes Suzette, that famous culinary classic, makes a delectable finale to a special meal. This is my personal adaptation of the traditional recipe, slightly lighter and less rich than the original. The gently heated orange sauce balances beautifully with the fresh nectarines inside the crêpes.

Mix the orange peel with 1 tablespoon of the Canderel

---

finely grated peel and juice of 2 large oranges

---

4 tbs Canderel Spoonful

---

175 g (6 oz) sunflower margarine

---

4 tbs Grand Marnier

---

12 Basic Crêpes (see page 125)

---

350 g (12 oz) nectarines, stoned and sliced

Spoonful. Cream the margarine with the rest of the Canderel Spoonful. Put the orange juice into a small saucepan and heat gently. Add the

creamed margarine and heat very gently until melted. Off the heat, stir in the Grand Marnier and the grated peel.

Brush each crêpe with a little warm sauce. Put a pile of sliced nectarines into the centre, and wrap it over to make a little parcel. Spoon the rest of the sauce over the top of the 12 parcels and serve at once on warm plates.

GINGERED PEACH SOUFFLÉ-OMELETTE

SERVES 4

I happen to be mad about ginger, so this elegant dessert is a personal favourite and has never failed to delight my friends.

Cut the prepared peaches into thin

---

3 ripe peaches, peeled and stoned

---

1 tsp lemon juice

---

2 tbs clear honey

---

50 g (2 oz) stem ginger, diced finely

---

1 tsp ground ginger

Basic Soufflé-Omelette (see page 125)

Heat the oven to Gas Mark 7/ 220°C/425°F.

---

slices and mix them with the lemon juice and honey. Mix in the diced stem ginger and the ground ginger. Spread this filling over the top of the omelette just before folding it over and putting it back in the oven.

CRÊPES AU MOKA

SERVES 6

These crêpes are made with a touch of both coffee and cocoa in the pancake batter, and they are filled with a light coffee-flavoured crème fraîche and sliced fruit. A delicious dinner-party dessert.

Mix the crème fraîche or Greek yogurt with the Canderel Spoonful

500 g (1 lb) crème fraîche or Greek yogurt
6 tbs Canderel Spoonful
2 tbs strong black coffee
2 egg whites
6 satsumas, peeled and divided into segments *or* 6 peaches, peeled, stoned and sliced
12 Basic Crêpes made with 1 tbs cocoa powder and 1 tbs coffee powder added to the flour (see page 125)

and stir in the coffee. Beat the egg whites stiffly then fold them in evenly and lightly.

To fill the pancakes, put a row of satsuma segments or peach slices down the centre of each crêpe, pile the flavoured crème on top and roll up. Decorate with extra slices of fruit and serve chilled.

GÂTEAU DE CRÊPES

SERVES 6–8

Layers of crêpes alternate with a delectable hazelnut mixture in this impressive cold dessert, which is surprisingly easy to make.

Blend the toasted hazelnuts in a liquidiser until finely ground and stir them into the cold Crème Patissière. Stiffly beat the egg whites, fold in

125 g (4 oz) hazelnuts, toasted
450 ml (¾ pint) Crème Patissière (see page 115)
3 tbs Canderel Spoonful
2 egg whites
12 Basic Crêpes (see page 125)
25 g (1 oz) flaked almonds, toasted
1 tbs clear honey, warmed

the Canderel Spoonful, then beat again until really thick and glossy. Fold into the hazelnut crème.

Make layers of crêpes sandwiched with the hazelnut crème, finishing with a crêpe for the top layer. Sprinkle with the almonds, then drizzle with the honey. Serve as soon as possible, cut into wedges.

NUT SOUFFLÉ PANCAKES
SERVES 6

Very delicate in flavour, these crêpes are made with the addition of a little grated orange peel in the batter mixture, while the nuts in the filling give this lovely dessert a delectable crunchiness.

Whisk the egg yolks with the honey and beat in the flour. Add the milk, and beat until smooth. Stir in the

2 egg yolks
2 tbs clear honey
40 g (1½ oz) plain flour
250 ml (8 fl oz) skimmed milk
125 g (4 oz) flaked almonds, toasted
4 egg whites
12 Basic Crêpes made with the grated peel of 1 orange added to the batter (see page 125)
TO DECORATE:
a little Canderel Spoonful
strips of orange peel
Heat the oven to Gas Mark 7/ 220°C/425°F.

almonds, then beat the egg whites very stiffly and fold in. Pile some of the mixture on to the centre of each crêpe, roll it up and place in a very large greased baking dish. Bake in the oven for 10 minutes, sprinkle with Canderel Spoonful and serve immediately, decorated with twists of orange peel.

RASPBERRY SOUFFLÉ-OMELETTE
SERVES 4

Basically you can put any seasonal summer fruits inside a soufflé-omelette and none of them needs pre-cooking. So in this recipe you can substitute apricots, strawberries, mangoes, pineapple or kiwifruit for the raspberries. But I think raspberries harmonise to perfection with the lightness of a soufflé-omelette.

Put the raspberries into a bowl and

350 g (12 oz) raspberries, hulled
2 tbs clear honey, warmed
Basic Soufflé-Omelette (see page 125)
a little Canderel Spoonful
Heat the oven to Gas Mark 7/ 220°C/425°F.

trickle the honey over them. Mix well and leave for 10 minutes while you prepare the soufflé-omelette. Spread the raspberries over the top just before folding and putting it back in the oven. Sprinkle with the Canderel Spoonful just before serving.

Nut Soufflé Pancakes (page 44); Raspberry Soufflé-omelette (page 44)

APPLE CRÊPE CAKE
SERVES 6

Warming food for autumn, when apples are plentiful, this is nourishing family fare. Serve it warm in the first chilly weekends as summer fades.

Put the apples into a deep, heavy saucepan with the lemon peel and a little water. Cook over a low heat, covered, shaking the pan from time to time, until the apples are completely soft. Stir occasionally with a wooden spoon. Cool a little,

8 large dessert apples, peeled, cored and sliced
grated peel of 1 lemon
4 tbs Canderel Spoonful
½ teaspoon grated nutmeg
2 tsp vanilla essence
50 g (2 oz) mixed chopped peel
12 Basic Crêpes (see page 125), kept warm
Apricot Sauce (see page 116)
50 g (2 oz) flaked almonds, toasted

then add the Canderel Spoonful, nutmeg and vanilla, and blend to a purée in a liquidiser. Stir in the chopped peel.

Place one crêpe on a large serving dish and spread thinly with apple purée. Cover with the next crêpe, and continue this process until all the purée and crêpes are used up, leaving the top crêpe uncovered. Spoon a little Apricot Sauce over the top and pour the rest around the edge. Sprinkle the almonds over the top and serve.

FRESH-FRUIT CRÊPES
SERVES 6

A perfect dessert for a summer's day, these light crêpes, filled with seasonal fruits and brushed with a honey glaze, are delicious served with Yogurt Dessert Sauce (see page 117).

Mix the prepared fruits with the lemon juice and sweeten to taste with the Canderel Spoonful.

350 g (12 oz) peaches, peeled and sliced thinly
350 g (12 oz) mixed strawberries and raspberries, hulled
1 tbs lemon juice
2–3 tbs Canderel Spoonful
3 tbs clear honey
40 g (1½ oz) sunflower margarine
12 Basic Crêpes (see page 125), kept warm

In a small saucepan combine the honey with the margarine and stir over a gentle heat until the honey has dissolved. Set aside.

To serve, spread some of the prepared fruit on each crêpe and roll up. Brush the top with the honey mixture and grill lightly until browned.

Country Crêpes (page 48); Fresh Fruit Crêpes (page 46); Apple Crêpe Cake (page 46)

COUNTRY CRÊPES

SERVES 4

My children adore pancakes, and so over the years I have had to concoct different ways of doing them. This is an autumnal version which goes down particularly well.

Cut the prepared apples into small

2 cooking apples (preferably Bramleys), peeled and cored
25 g (1 oz) walnuts, chopped
50 g (2 oz) raisins
4 tbs Canderel Spoonful
250 g (8 oz) Greek yogurt
8 Basic Crêpes (see page 125)

dice. Mix with the walnuts and raisins and 3 tablespoons of the Canderel Spoonful. Mix in the Greek yogurt thoroughly, and stuff the crêpes with this mixture. Serve chilled, with the rest of the Canderel Spoonful sprinkled over the top.

PEAR AND CHOCOLATE SOUFFLÉ-OMELETTE

SERVES 4

The combination of pears with chocolate is sublime, and makes a delectable filling for a soufflé-omelette.

Put the cocoa and cinnamon into a pan with the water and bring gently to simmering point, stirring thoroughly. Reduce the heat and poach the sliced pears and orange peel in the liquid for 5 minutes, until tender. Cool a little, then drain the fruit, reserving the liquid.

2 tsp cocoa powder
½ tsp cinnamon
150 ml (¼ pint) water
2 ripe dessert pears, peeled, cored and sliced
grated peel of 1 orange
Basic Soufflé-Omelette (see page 24)
50 g (2 oz) plain chocolate, grated
2 tbs Canderel Spoonful
4 tbs crème fraîche or fromage frais
Heat the oven to Gas Mark 7/ 220°C/425°F.

Make the soufflé-omelette, fill it with the pear slices and sprinkle over a quarter of the grated chocolate. Fold the omelette over and finish cooking.

Add the Canderel Spoonful to the cooking juices from the pears, and fold into the crème fraîche or fromage frais. Pour this sauce over the top of each helping. Sprinkle the rest of the grated chocolate over and serve immediately.

DELICATE ICES
AND
BOMBES

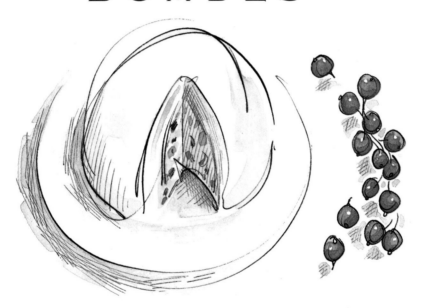

BASIC ICE CREAM
SERVES 6

This very simple ice cream is the basis for all of the ice creams that I have included here. They are all extremely light, made with crème fraîche instead of double cream, and egg whites instead of whole eggs. Although this is a 'basic' ice cream, it is delicious enough to serve as it stands, with any of the fruit sauces mentioned in the book.

500 g (1 lb) crème fraîche or double or whipping cream, whipped

6 tbs Canderel Spoonful

3 tsp vanilla essence

3 egg whites

Mix the crème fraîche or cream with the Canderel Spoonful and flavour with the vanilla essence. Beat the egg whites stiffly and fold in very thoroughly, and pour into a freezerproof container. Cover and freeze for 5–6 hours.

RASPBERRY ICE CREAM
SERVES 6

A beautiful dark-pink ice cream with a delicate flavour, this is a regular favourite of mine for dinner parties and family meals alike. It has a fresh, summery fruitiness that is instantly appealing.

Blend the raspberries thoroughly in a liquidiser. Pass through a sieve to separate the pulp from the pips.

350 g (12 oz) raspberries, hulled

6 tbs Canderel Spoonful

500 g (1 lb) crème fraîche or double or whipping cream, whipped

2 tsp vanilla essence

2 egg whites

Sweeten with 2 tablespoons of the Canderel Spoonful.

Mix the crème fraîche or cream with the rest of the Canderel Spoonful, and flavour with the vanilla essence. Mix into the raspberry purée and blend thoroughly with a wooden spoon. Then beat the egg whites stiffly and fold them in. Put into a freezerproof container. Cover and freeze for 5–6 hours.

Apricot Macaroon Ice Cream (page 52); Brown-bread Ice (page 52); Raspberry Ice Cream (page 50)

APRICOT MACAROON ICE CREAM
SERVES 6

I am wild about this ice cream – the almondy flavour of the macaroons blends beautifully with the fresh apricots, and the crushed biscuits give the ice cream an irresistible texture.

Put the apricots into a bowl and pour boiling water over them. Soak for a minute, then drain and peel them.

350 g (12 oz) ripe apricots
1 tbs lemon juice
6 tbs Canderel Spoonful
250 g (8 oz) crème fraîche or double or whipping cream, whipped
2 egg whites
125 g (4 oz) Italian macaroons, crushed

Cut in half and remove the stones. Put into a liquidiser with the lemon juice, and blend to a purée. Stir in half of the Canderel Spoonful.

Mix the crème fraîche or cream with the rest of the Canderel Spoonful and then stir the two mixtures together thoroughly. Beat the egg whites stiffly, then fold them in, then fold in the crushed macaroons. Put into a freezerproof container, cover and freeze for 5–6 hours.

BROWN-BREAD ICE
SERVES 4

A quaint-sounding idea, this is based on a traditional English recipe and is surprisingly good. It should be eaten a few hours after it is made, as it requires just a light freezing.

In a large, shallow baking dish, crisp the breadcrumbs in the preheated oven for 20–30 minutes, shaking them from time to time so that they

50 g (2 oz) fresh brown breadcrumbs
250 g (8 oz) crème fraîche or fromage frais
4 tbs Canderel Spoonful
2 tbs freshly squeezed orange juice
2 tsp lemon juice
2 egg whites
Heat the oven to Gas Mark 2/ 150°C/300°F.

brown evenly. Set aside to cool.

Mash the crème fraîche or fromage frais with the Canderel Spoonful and stir in the orange juice and the lemon juice. Fold in the cooled, crisp breadcrumbs, then beat the egg whites stiffly and fold in. Put into a freezerproof container, cover and freeze for about 2–3 hours, until lightly set.

TUTTI-FRUTTI ICE CREAM
SERVES 4

This recipe was given to my mother by one of the chefs in the Cambridge college where we lived during my childhood. Chopped glacé fruits mixed with pistachio nuts give this light ice cream their own peculiar flavour and texture – and it is an ice cream for any time of the year.

75 g (3 oz) raisins
3 tbs rum or kirsch
250 g (8 oz) crème fraîche or fromage frais
4 tbs Canderel Spoonful
2 tsp vanilla essence
50 g (2 oz) glacé cherries, sliced
25 g (1 oz) angelica, chopped
25 g (1 oz) stem ginger, chopped
25 g (1 oz) pistachio nuts, toasted lightly
2 egg whites

Soak the raisins in the rum or kirsch for half an hour. Mix the crème fraîche or fromage frais with the Canderel Spoonful and flavour with the vanilla. Add the prepared fruits and nuts and mix in well. Beat the egg whites stiffly and fold them in. Pour into a freezerproof container, cover and freeze for 5–6 hours.

CHAMPAGNE SORBET
SERVES 6

A palate-freshener, this silvery champagne sorbet can be sampled in-between courses, or at the end of a rich meal.

Mix the champagne with the fruit juices. Put into a freezerproof container, cover and freeze, stirring

600 ml (1 pint) champagne or sparkling white wine
juice of 2 lemons
juice of 1 orange
250 g (8 oz) crème fraîche or fromage frais
6 tbs Canderel Spoonful

from time to time as the edges begin

to set. Mix the crème fraîche or fromage frais with the Canderel Spoonful. While the sorbet is still mushy and not completely frozen, stir in the sweetened crème fraîche. Return to the freezer, cover and allow to freeze completely, which will take 5–6 hours.

Bombe Chateaubriand (page 58); Champagne Sorbet (page 53); Tutti-frutti Ice Cream (page 53); Pineapple Moka Ice en Surprise

(page 59)

FROZEN ALMOND CREAMS

SERVES 4—6

Individual dishes of this almond-flavoured, nutty ice cream make a lovely dessert course for a party. Toasted almonds have rich and pungent flavour, so a small serving is all that is required – and a cup of good coffee to follow.

Beat the egg whites until frothy, and fold in the Canderel Spoonful. Beat

2 egg whites
4 tbs Canderel Spoonful
125 g (4 oz) chopped almonds, toasted
250 g (8 oz) crème fraîche or double or whipping cream, whipped
a few drops of almond essence

again until the mixture is thick and stiff.

Reserve a few of the almonds for decoration, then fold the rest into the crème fraîche or cream quickly and evenly. Stir in the almond essence, then fold in the stiffly beaten egg whites. Spoon into individual freezerproof dishes. Cover and freeze for 2–3 hours before serving, sprinkled with the reserved almonds.

FROZEN FRUIT YOGURT

SERVES 6

Freezing yogurt is a brilliant idea – you can improvise with your favourite fruits, add fruit juices, and try folding in nuts too. These frozen yogurts are fresher than traditional ice creams, lighter and very refreshing.

Prepare the ripe fruit, then liquidise to make 300 ml (½ pint) fruit purée.

350 g (12 oz) ripe fruit (apricots, bananas, guavas, mangoes, peaches, strained raspberries or blackberries, pineapple or strawberries)
1 tsp grated lemon peel
1 tbs lemon juice
2 tbs Canderel Spoonful
600 ml (1 pint) natural yogurt
1 egg white

Add the lemon peel and juice and Canderel Spoonful to the liquidiser,

and blend again. Stir into the yogurt and mix thoroughly. Beat the egg white stiffly and fold in. Put into a freezerproof container, cover and freeze.

Allow to soften a little at room temperature before serving, and use up within 2–3 days, otherwise the yogurt tends to crystallise.

Frozen Fruit Yogurts (page 56): Banana, Kiwi and Strawberry; Frozen Almond Creams

BOMBE CHATEAUBRIAND
SERVES 6

Traditionally, as here, a bombe is made by lining a bombe mould with a light ice cream or water ice, filling the centre with a 'mousse', and freezing. Bombes make spectacular puddings, because they can combine both lovely colours and textures. They take dedication to achieve, but the results are worth it. This is a healthier version of a famous French classic, devised by Montmireil, chef to Chateaubriand.

Simmer the apricots in the orange juice gently until tender – about 5 minutes. Leave to cool, then liquidise to a purée. Add the lemon juice and sweeten with the Canderel

FOR THE LINING:

500 g (1 lb) ripe apricots, peeled, stoned and halved

300 ml (½ pint) orange juice

juice of half a lemon

3 tbs Canderel Spoonful

FOR THE FILLING:

75 g (3 oz) mixed glacé fruits, chopped

2 tbs kirsch

2 eggs, separated

2 tbs clear honey

1 tbs cornflour

300 ml (½ pint) skimmed milk, warmed

2 tsp vanilla essence

125 g (4 oz) crème fraîche, mashed

Spoonful. Pour into a bombe mould or soufflé dish, cover and freeze. When almost frozen, hollow it out

by pressing the ice from the centre against the sides of the mould or dish in order to line it. Cover and refreeze.

To make the filling, soak the glacé fruits in the kirsch. Beat the egg yolks with the honey and stir in the cornflour. Gradually add the warmed milk, stirring all the time. Return to the pan and stir over a gentle heat until it thickens. Allow to cool. Stir in the vanilla and fold in the crème fraîche. Fold in the glacé fruits and kirsch. Stiffly beat the egg whites then fold into the mixture. Pour into the lined bombe mould, cover and freeze for 5–6 hours. Invert onto a plate to serve.

MANGO ICE CREAM
SERVES 4–6

One of the best ice creams in the world. Its delicate yet distinctive flavour is sublime. Serve it at a special dinner party.

Purée the fruit in a liquidiser. Mix the crème fraîche or cream with the

350 g (12 oz) fresh mango flesh

250 g (8 oz) crème fraîche or double or whipping cream, whipped

4 tbs Canderel Spoonful

2 tsp vanilla essence

2 egg whites

Canderel Spoonful and flavour with the vanilla. Mix in the mango purée and blend thoroughly. Beat the egg whites stiffly and fold in. Pour into a freezerproof container. Cover and freeze for 5–6 hours.

PINEAPPLE MOKA ICE EN SURPRISE
SERVES 4–6

Serve this pineapple shell filled with alternate layers of fresh, chopped pineapple and coffee ice cream when you want a really spectacular dessert.

Cut the top off the pineapple and reserve the leafy head. Hollow out the fruit without damaging the skin, and chop it finely. Mix with 2 tablespoons of the Canderel

1 large ripe pineapple
6 tbs Canderel Spoonful
500 g (1 lb) crème fraîche or double or whipping cream, whipped
3 tbs very strong black coffee
2 egg whites

Spoonful and chill in the fridge.

Mix the crème fraîche or cream with the rest of the Canderel Spoonful and mix in the black coffee.

Beat the egg whites stiffly and fold in evenly. Pour into a freezerproof container and freeze, for 5–6 hours.

To assemble, put a layer of the ice cream in the bottom of the pineapple shell, cover with a layer of the chopped fruit, and continue making layers until the shell is full. Cover and freeze until ready to serve, and dish up with the top of the pineapple replaced.

RASPBERRY FROST
SERVES 6

This is a dessert with a difference: crushed raspberry sorbet is folded into crème Chantilly just before serving.

Purée the raspberries in a liquidiser and press through a sieve to remove the pips. Stir the lemon juice into the pulp, and sweeten with 2 tablespoons of the Canderel Spoonful. Put into a shallow freezerproof container and freeze

500 g (1 lb) raspberries, hulled
3 tsp lemon juice
6 tbs Canderel Spoonful
2 egg whites
250 g (8 oz) crème fraîche or double or whipping cream, whipped
grated peel of half a lemon
sprigs of fresh mint, to decorate

until almost solid but still soft enough to crush or chop.

Stiffly beat the egg whites,

then fold in the rest of the Canderel Spoonful and continue beating until very stiff indeed. Mix the crème fraîche or cream with the lemon peel and fold in the beaten egg whites.

Chop or crush the half-frozen raspberry sorbet into bite-sized pieces, and fold into the crème fraîche mixture so that it makes a 'ripple' effect. Serve at once, in tall glasses, decorated with little sprigs of fresh mint.

MARQUISE À L'ANANAS
SERVES 4–6

Fresh pineapple makes one of the most successful of home-made ice creams. Piled into the shell before freezing, this ice makes a stylish dessert for a supper party.

Cut the pineapple in half lengthways and scoop out the pulp carefully, without breaking the shell and retaining as much of the juice as

1 large pineapple
2 egg whites
4 tbs Canderel Spoonful
250 g (8 oz) crème fraîche or fromage frais
grated peel and juice of 1 lemon

possible. Remove the woody core, and purée the rest of the fruit and juices to a pulp.

Beat the egg whites until they are frothy, then fold in

2 tablespoons of the Canderel Spoonful and beat again until very stiff. Mash the crème fraîche or fromage frais with the rest of the Canderel Spoonful, and add the pineapple pulp, the lemon juice and peel. Fold in the egg-white mixture quickly and evenly. Pile back into the pineapple shells, cover and freeze for 5–6 hours.

ICED SOUFFLÉ
SERVES 4

For all its simplicity, this iced soufflé is wonderfully light and fresh. During spring and summer I like to decorate it with a sprig of flowering herb, or a nasturtium flower or two.

Prepare a soufflé dish (see page 24). Blend the fruit to a purée in a liquidiser, and stir in the lemon juice.

350 g (12 oz) fresh fruit (apricots, mangoes, peaches, raspberries or strawberries), prepared
1 tbs lemon juice
2 eggs, separated
3 tbs Canderel Spoonful
250 g (8 oz) Greek yogurt
herbs or flowers, to decorate

Beat the egg yolks with the Canderel Spoonful until pale and creamy, then beat in the Greek yogurt. Fold in the fruit purée.

Beat the egg whites until they are very stiff, and fold them into the mixture. Pour into a freezerproof container, cover and freeze for at least 4 hours.

Marquise à l'Ananas (page 60)

PEACH AND ORANGE SORBET

SERVES 6–8

A friend gave me this recipe years ago, and I have used it over and over again. People invariably expect that it has to be made in a sorbetière, but in fact it doesn't – the method is simplicity itself.

---

500 g (1 lb) ripe peaches, peeled and stoned

---

300 ml (½ pint) fresh orange juice

3–4 tbs Canderel Spoonful

---

2 tsp lemon juice

Put the prepared fruit and the orange juice into a liquidiser and blend to a purée. Add the Canderel Spoonful to taste, and the lemon juice. Pour into a freezerproof container, cover and freeze for 1 hour, then stir thoroughly and refreeze for 5–6 hours.

SUMMER-FRUITS BOMBE

SERVES 6

There are as many ways of making bombes as there are ice-cream and sorbet recipes; improvisation is the name of the game. This one conjures up high summer, and should be eaten al fresco on a balmy summer's evening.

Let the sorbet soften a little, then

⅔ quantity Peach and Orange Sorbet mixture (see above)

Basic Ice Cream (see page 50)

---

125 g (4 oz) strawberries, hulled and chopped finely

---

125 g (4 oz) raspberries, hulled

---

125 g (4 oz) blackcurrants, topped and tailed

4–6 tbs Canderel Spoonful

---

line a large bombe mould with it, pressing it around the bottom and edges of the mould evenly. Refreeze.

Put the prepared fruits into a bowl and mix with the Canderel Spoonful to taste. Fold with all their juices into the basic ice cream mixture, pour into the prepared bombe mould and freeze for 5–6 hours.

THE
BEST OF FAMILY
DESSERTS
AND
CRUMBLES

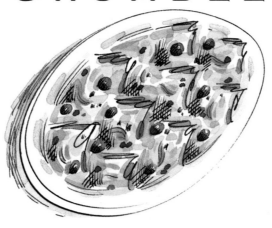

MINCE PIES

MAKES 24

Traditional mincemeat is made with suet and sugar added, but I have devised this way of making it with fruit and Canderel only, so that all the fruit flavours emerge fresh and well defined. Store the mixture in the fridge, and use within a day or two, because it doesn't keep well. But it can be frozen if you want to make it in advance.

Mix the fruits and spices together in a large bowl, then blend thoroughly in a liquidiser, a little at a time.

125 g (4 oz) currants
125 g (4 oz) raisins
125 g (4 oz) sultanas
50 g (2 oz) dried dates
50 g (2 oz) mixed peel
50 g (2 oz) glacé cherries
50 g (2 oz) flaked almonds
1 ripe banana, mashed
4 tbs brandy or fresh orange juice
½ tsp ground ginger
½ tsp nutmeg
½ tsp mixed spice
500 g (1 lb) Sweet Crust Pastry (see page 124)
1 egg, beaten
a little Canderel Spoonful
Heat the oven to Gas Mark 4/ 180°C/350°F.

Keep chilled.

Roll out the pastry, then cut out 24 rounds with a large fluted cutter and another 24 rounds with a smaller cutter. Line 24 bun tins with the larger rounds. Fill with mincemeat. Dampen the pastry edges and place small pastry rounds on top. Brush the tops with beaten egg, and bake for 10–12 minutes in the oven, until the pies are crisp and golden brown. Cool on a rack before lifting carefully out of the tins.

Fresh-fruit Trifle (page 66); Winter Pudding (page 67); Mince Pies (page 64)

FRESH-FRUIT TRIFLE

SERVES 4—6

A versatile family favourite, trifle can be made with all kinds of fruit, according to taste. The Italians call it *Zuppa Inglese* which always seems to me to be rather impolite; it is far from soupy. With its fresh-fruit flavours and smooth creamy custard topping, it is irresistible.

Prepare the Crème Patissière and allow to cool for 20 minutes. Cut the trifle sponges in half lengthways and lay in the bottom of a 23 cm (9-inch) round soufflé dish. Sprinkle with the tropical-fruit juice and set to one side. Mix the prepared and sliced fruits with 3—4 tablespoons of the Canderel Spoonful in a separate bowl.

Spoon the fruits over the sponge layer, and cover with the Crème Patissière. Chill for several hours, or overnight. Just before serving, mix the crème fraîche or Greek yogurt with the remaining Canderel Spoonful, beat the egg white stiffly and fold in. Smother the top of the trifle with this mixture, and decorate with the grated chocolate and strips of angelica.

600 ml (1 pint) Crème Patissière (see page 115)

4 trifle sponge cakes

5 tbs tropical-fruit juice

750 g (1½ lb) fresh fruit (starfruit, bananas, strawberries, mangoes, kiwifruit, oranges, peaches, pears, grapes), prepared and sliced

6—7 tbs Canderel Spoonful

250 g (8 oz) crème fraîche or Greek yogurt

1 egg white

TO DECORATE:

plain chocolate, grated

angelica strips

WINTER PUDDING

SERVES 6

Summer Pudding (see page 22) is an all-round favourite among classic puddings, and a winter version always goes down well in my family. I use dried fruits and soak them in aromatic tea, and the resulting pudding is festive, nourishing and warming.

Prepare the fruit: if using whole fruits, stone them and chop them to the size of raisins. Put into a large bowl with the spices and lemon peel, pour over the hot tea and leave to soak overnight.

Remove the crusts from the

500 g (1 lb) mixed dried fruits (apricots, prunes, dates, raisins, sultanas)
7.5 cm (3-inch) stick of cinnamon
4 cloves
¼ tsp grated nutmeg
7.5 cm (3-inch) strip of lemon peel
1.2 litres (2 pints) Earl Grey tea
10-12 large slices wholemeal bread

bread, and cut 6 slices in half lengthways. Line the sides of a greased 20 cm (8-inch) cake tin or mould with these. Cut the rest of the bread into triangles and fit some of them over the base of the tin so that it is completely covered.

Remove the whole spices and the lemon peel from the fruit, and spoon the fruit into the lined tin, adding some of the juices so that the bread is well moistened. Fit the remaining bread triangles over the top, and trim the sides. Pour more juices over the pudding to moisten all the bread.

Cover with greaseproof paper and weight the pudding down with a heavy object. Chill overnight and, when ready to serve, invert it into a shallow serving dish and offer it around with Greek yogurt or crème fraîche.

RASPBERRY AND STRAWBERRY ZINGARA

SERVES 4

A purée of strawberries flavoured with orange and mixed with crème fraîche is poured over whole raspberries in a glass bowl. Simple to make, this is a family dessert for a special, summery occasion.

Purée the strawberries in a liquidiser. Pour the orange juice

350 g (12 oz) strawberries, hulled
finely grated peel and juice of 1 large orange
6 tbs Canderel Spoonful
350 g (12 oz) crème fraîche or fromage frais
350 g (12 oz) raspberries, hulled

over the prepared strawberries. Mix

in 2 tablespoons of the Canderell Spoonful.

Mash the crème fraîche or fromage frais with the rest of the Canderel Spoonful and mix in the finely grated orange peel. Fold the crème into the strawberry purée. Put the raspberries into a glass bowl and pour the cream over the top. Chill.

Blackberry Grunt (page 71); Raspberry and Strawberry Zingara (page 67); Pineapple Peach Cobbler (page 70)

PINEAPPLE PEACH COBBLER

SERVES 6

The sight of this fruit cobbler produces delighted faces around the table in my family. It is a really tasty pudding – satisfying without being heavy. It takes a little time to prepare but it is worth every minute.

For the dough, sift the flour with the cornflour and salt, and crumble in the margarine lightly. Add the water and honey. Mix well together and knead lightly. Line a well-greased, deep dish about 18 × 28 cm (7 × 11 inches) with three-quarters of the pastry, reserving enough for the top lattice. Bake the pastry shell for 10 minutes in the oven, then leave to cool on a rack. Reduce the

---

FOR THE DOUGH:

250 g (8 oz) plain flour

25 g (1 oz) cornflour

½ tsp salt

175 g (6 oz) sunflower margarine

1 tbs water

1 tbs clear honey, warmed

FOR THE FILLING:

4–6 tbs clear honey

2 tbs cornflour

25 g (1 oz) sunflower margarine

300 ml (½ pint) pineapple juice

½ tsp ground nutmeg

½ tsp ground cinnamon

1 tsp grated lemon peel

2 tsp lemon juice

350 g (12 oz) fresh peeled and cored pineapple

350 g (12 oz) peaches, peeled, stoned and sliced

Heat the oven to Gas Mark 8/ 230°C/450°F.

---

oven temperature to Gas Mark 3/ 160°C/325°F.

For the filling, mix the honey, cornflour, margarine and pineapple juice in a saucepan, and cook gently until thick, stirring all the time – about 5 minutes. Add the spices, lemon peel and juice. Pour over the prepared fruits in a bowl, and mix well together. Spoon the filling evenly into the pastry shell, and criss-cross the top with strips of the remaining pastry.

Return to the oven and bake for 40–45 minutes, until golden brown all over. Cool on a rack for 10 minutes. Serve warm, with crème fraîche or Greek yogurt.

BLACKBERRY GRUNT
SERVES 6

The name of this pudding is immediately appealing – and so is the pudding itself. Succulent ripe blackberries topped with a light golden dough – wonderful family food for an autumn weekend.

Put the blackberries into a large soufflé dish with the warm honey, and mix them together well.

For the topping, sift the dry ingredients together and lightly rub

1 kg (2 lb) ripe blackberries, hulled
4 tbs clear honey, warmed
FOR THE TOPPING:
250 g (8 oz) plain flour
4 tsp baking powder
1 tsp salt
25 g (1 oz) sunflower margarine
150 ml (¼ pint) skimmed milk
Heat the oven to Gas Mark 6/ 200°C/400°F.

in the margarine. Stir in the milk quickly and knead until light. Roll out on a well-floured surface, to a round the same circumference as the dish, and about 2 cm (¾ inch) thick. Place the dough over the top of the fruit, and bake in the oven for 25–30 minutes until the topping is well-risen and golden. Serve hot, with crème fraîche or Crème Anglaise (see page 120).

ORANGE AND HAZELNUT CRUMBLE

SERVES 6

Fruit crumbles are staple food in my family, popular throughout the year. Here is one with a biscuit-crumb topping and an unusual combination of oranges and hazelnuts. I like to serve it with either Greek yogurt or Crème Anglaise (see page 120).

Make layers of the orange segments in a soufflé dish, sprinkling each layer with some chopped hazelnuts.

---

4 medium oranges, peeled and segmented

---

75 g (3 oz) hazelnuts, chopped

2–3 tbs clear honey, warmed

---

350 g (12 oz) digestive-biscuit crumbs

---

75 g (3 oz) plain flour, sifted

½ tsp bicarbonate of soda

---

1 tsp ground ginger

---

150 g (5 oz) sunflower margarine

---

a little Canderel Spoonful

Heat the oven to Gas Mark 4/ 180°C/350°F.

Pour the warmed honey over the top of the orange and nuts.

Mix the biscuit crumbs with the sifted flour, bicarbonate of soda and ginger. Lightly rub the margarine into the crumbs, until crumbly. Sprinkle over the fruit in the dish, and bake in the oven for 25 minutes, until the top is lightly browned and crisp. Sprinkle with a little Canderel Spoonful just before serving.

APRICOT ALMOND CRUMBLE

SERVES 4—6

The macaroon topping on this crumble complements the apricots in its base. Serve hot with Crème Chantilly (see page 116).

Put the prepared apricots into the bottom of an ovenproof dish and mix with the blanched almonds. Trickle the honey over the top.

---

750 g (1½ lb) ripe apricots, stoned and sliced

---

125 g (4 oz) blanched almonds, halved

---

3 tbs clear honey, warmed

FOR THE TOPPING:

250 g (8 oz) macaroon crumbs

---

65 g (2½ oz) plain flour, sifted

---

1 tsp baking powder

---

75 g (3 oz) sunflower margarine

Heat the oven to Gas Mark 4/ 180°C/350°F.

Mix the macaroon crumbs with the sifted flour and baking powder, and lightly rub in the margarine. Sprinkle over the top of the fruit. Press down gently and bake in the oven for 20 minutes, until the top is lightly browned and crisp.

Best Apple Crunch (page 74); Orange and Hazelnut Crumble (page 72); Apricot Almond Crumble (page 72)

BREAD AND BUTTER PUDDING

SERVES 6

There are probably as many versions of bread and butter pudding as there are good English cooks. At its best it is an exquisite pudding. In this recipe I have included apricots along with the traditional fruit, raisins.

Trim the crusts from the bread. Butter the slices and cut each one in half diagonally. Arrange these slices in a well-buttered baking dish,

10 thin slices wholemeal bread
50 g (2 oz) sunflower margarine
350 g (12 oz) ripe apricots, stoned and sliced
75 g (3 oz) raisins
2 eggs
300 ml (½ pint) skimmed milk, warmed
coarsely grated peel of 1 orange
1 tsp vanilla essence
Heat the oven to Gas Mark 5/ 190°C/375°F.

alternating the layers with the apricots and raisins, ending with a bread layer.

Beat the eggs thoroughly, then stir in the warm milk and the orange peel. Flavour with the vanilla essence. Pour over the top of the buttered bread and bake in the oven for 40 minutes, until the pudding is set and golden brown. Serve hot or warm, with Greek yogurt.

BEST APPLE CRUNCH

SERVES 4

My family loves this mouthwatering crunch served with Crème Anglaise (see page 120).

Toss the apple slices with the lemon juice, honey, spices and melted margarine. Mix well and put into a baking dish.

To make the topping, sift the

500 g (1 lb) dessert apples, peeled and sliced
2 tsp lemon juice
1–2 tbs clear honey, warmed
1 tsp ground cinnamon
1 tsp ground nutmeg
40 g (1½ oz) sunflower margarine, melted
FOR THE TOPPING:
125 g (4 oz) plain flour
2 tsp mixed spice
125 g (4 oz) sunflower margarine
125 g (4 oz) porridge oats
50 g (2 oz) walnuts, chopped
2 tbs clear honey, warmed
a little Canderel Spoonful
Heat the oven to Gas Mark 5/ 190°C/375°F.

flour with the spice and lightly rub in the margarine. Stir in the oats, the nuts and the honey. Sprinkle over the top of the apples and bake in the oven for 20–25 minutes, until the topping is lightly browned and crisp. Cool on a rack for 5 minutes, sprinkle the top with a little Canderel Spoonful, and serve.

Eighteenth-century Trifle (page 76); Bread and Butter Pudding (page 74); Spicy Carrot Cake (page 76)

EIGHTEENTH-CENTURY TRIFLE
SERVES 4

Traditionally trifles were made with ratafias soaked in sherry, then spread with strawberry or raspberry jam and topped with thick cream. In this recipe, the soaked ratafias are simply topped with a light syllabub mixture – plain but delicious.

250 g (8 oz) ratafias or little Italian macaroons, crushed
4 tbs Grand Marnier or brandy
4 tbs Canderel Spoonful
500 g (1 lb) crème fraîche or Greek yogurt
5 tbs fresh orange juice
5 tbs lemon juice

Soak the ratafias or macaroons in the liqueur. Mix the Canderel Spoonful into the crème fraîche or Greek yogurt and gradually add the fruit juices, stirring all the time. Put the soaked ratafias or macaroons in the bottom of a serving dish, and cover with the crème. Chill overnight, so that it sets firmly.

SPICY CARROT CAKE
SERVES 6–8

A sumptuous, nourishing pudding which is definitely winter food, this version of carrot cake is enriched with the unlikely but successful combination of ground almonds and grated chocolate.

Beat the egg yolks with the honey until the mixture is pale and thick.

3 eggs, separated
3 tbs clear honey
250 g (8 oz) carrots, grated finely
50 g (2 oz) apple, peeled and grated finely
50 g (2 oz) sultanas
50 g (2 oz) raisins
grated peel and juice of 1 orange
grated peel and juice of 1 lemon
150 g (5 oz) ground almonds
50 g (2 oz) hazelnuts, ground coarsely
125 g (4 oz) sponge finger crumbs
50 g (2 oz) plain chocolate, grated
1 tsp ground cinnamon
1 tsp ground ginger
1 tsp mixed spice
Heat the oven to Gas Mark 4/ 180°C/350°F.

Whisk the egg whites stiffly. Stir all the remaining ingredients into the egg yolks, then fold in the egg whites. Turn the mixture into a well-greased 20 cm (8-inch) loose-bottomed cake tin and bake in the oven for 30–35 minutes.

Cool a little on a rack. Serve warm with Greek yogurt.

FRUIT SALADS
AND
COMPOTES

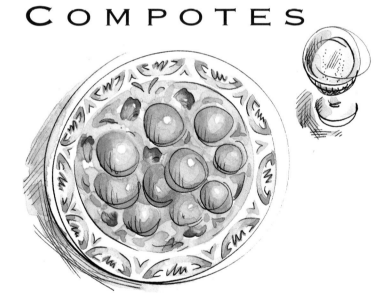

ORANGE CUPS
SERVES 4

A mouthwatering mixture of fruits simmered together in fruit juice and wine, then piled into orange skins.

Cut the oranges in half and scoop out the fruit with a grapefruit knife, without damaging the skins. Purée the fruit in a liquidiser, then put into a saucepan with the fruit juice and the sherry or white wine. Add the

2 large oranges
5 tbs tropical-fruit juice
2 tbs medium sherry or sweet white wine
1 banana, peeled and diced finely
1 thick slice pineapple, diced finely
125 g (4 oz) seedless grapes, peeled and halved
1 peach, peeled, stoned and diced
2 tbs Canderel Spoonful
1 egg white
125 g (4 oz) crème fraîche or fromage frais

rest of the prepared fruits, bring to boiling point and then simmer for 3 minutes. Pile into the orange cups. Allow to cool a little.

Beat the egg white until stiff, then fold in the Canderel Spoonful and beat again until very stiff. Fold into the crème fraîche or fromage frais and pile over the fruit. Serve at once.

ORANGE FLOWERS
SERVES 4

These oranges make a perfect dessert for a summer party or a buffet table. They are served with the segments opened out like flowers, and coated in a cognac-flavoured fruit sauce. Special food for a special occasion.

Put the orange juice into a small saucepan with the cornflour and orange peel, and heat gently, stirring all the time, until the mixture

150 ml (¼ pint) orange juice
1 tbs cornflour
1 tsp finely grated orange peel
2 tbs cognac
3–4 tbs Canderel Spoonful
15 g (½ oz) sunflower margarine
4 oranges
sprigs of mint, to decorate

thickens. Remove from the heat, cool a little and add the cognac and Canderel Spoonful. Stir in the

sunflower margarine.

Remove the peel and pith from the oranges and loosen the segments carefully down to the bottom, leaving them just joined at the base. Spread them out into a flower shape. Place in a glass dish and glaze with some of the sauce. Just before serving, pour the rest of the sauce over the oranges, and decorate with sprigs of mint.

Orange Cups (page 78); Orange Flowers (page 78)

PÊCHES AUX CASSIS
SERVES 6

When summer is at its height, I prefer to cook as simply as possible – not only in order to spend more time outdoors, but also to make the very best of the summer harvest of fresh fruit.

You can also make this dessert using mangoes, guavas or nectarines instead of the peaches.

Put the peaches into a bowl and pour

6 ripe peaches
2 tbs Canderel Spoonful
1 tbs lemon juice
2 tbs brandy
Hot Blackcurrant Sauce (see page 117)
250 g (8 oz) crème fraîche or double or whipping cream, whipped

boiling water over them. Leave for a minute or two, and then peel them.

Cut in half and remove the stones. Put into the bottom of a shallow glass dish, and sprinkle with the Canderel Spoonful and the lemon juice.

Add the brandy to the Hot Blackcurrant Sauce, and beat into the crème fraîche or cream. Spoon over the peaches in the dish, and chill for at least 2 hours before serving.

OGEN MELON WITH BLACKBERRIES
SERVES 4

When the first blackberries begin to ripen at the end of the summer, try them in this simple, fresh dessert: ogen melon halves filled with blackberries and topped with a scoop of ice cream.

Remove the seeds from the melon

2 ripe ogen melons, halved
4 tbs Canderel Spoonful
500 g (1 lb) ripe, sweet blackberries, hulled
4 scoops Basic Ice Cream (see page 50)

and sprinkle half of the Canderel Spoonful over the cut halves. Chill

in the fridge for 1–2 hours.

Mix the blackberries with the rest of the Canderel Spoonful and chill for 1–2 hours.

To serve, fill the melon halves with the blackberries and put a scoop of ice cream on top of each one. Serve immediately.

PEAR AND GRAPE COMPOTE
SERVES 4

Pale pears with light-green grapes make a most attractive compote, and the flavours of the fruit complement each other beautifully. Serve it with Crème Chantilly (see page 116).

Poach the pears in the orange juice and lemon juice for 8–10 minutes,

4 ripe, firm pears, peeled, cored and diced

300 ml (½ pint) orange juice

2 tsp lemon juice

175 g (6 oz) green seedless grapes, halved

2 tsp vanilla essence

3–4 tbs Canderel Spoonful

slivered almonds, toasted, to decorate

until soft but not mushy. The time will depend on the ripeness of the pears. Mix in the prepared grapes.

Allow to cool, then add the vanilla essence and sweeten with the Canderel Spoonful. Chill. Serve sprinkled with the toasted slivered almonds.

RHUBARB AND BANANA COMPOTE
SERVES 4

This is a really useful recipe, loved especially by children. Serve with Crème Anglaise (see page 120).

Trim the rhubarb and cut it into 2.5 cm (1-inch) lengths. Put into a casserole dish with the water and cook in the oven for 20 minutes,

500 g (1 lb) rhubarb

150 ml (¼ pint) water

juice of 1 orange

5 tbs Canderel Spoonful

3 bananas, peeled and sliced thinly

Heat the oven to Gas Mark 4/ 180°C/350°F.

until very tender. Allow to cool, then add the orange juice and sweeten with the Canderel Spoonful.

Put the sliced bananas in the bottom of a serving dish. Spoon the warm rhubarb over the top and leave to cool completely, then chill.

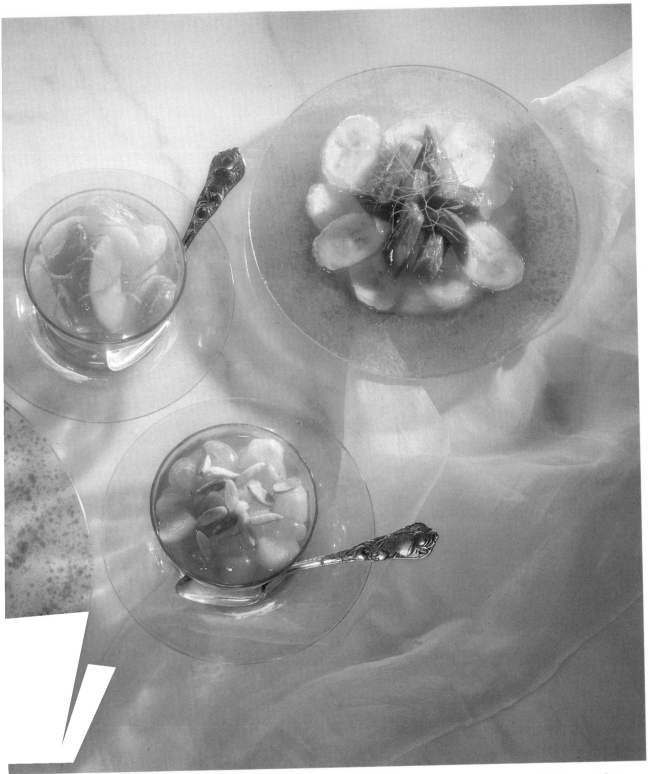

Ogen Melon with Blackberries (page 80); Pêches aux Cassis (page 80); Apple and Tangerine Compote (page 88); Pear and Grape Compote (page 81); Rhubarb and Banana Compote (page 81)

MACEDOINE OF FRUITS

SERVES 6—8

This is simply a fruit salad made with fruit juice or sweet white wine then left to marinate so that all the flavours develop. It is delicious with Lemon Sauce (see page 115), or you can serve it with Crème Chantilly (see page 116) or simply with Greek yogurt. During summer I like to decorate it with leaves of sweet cicely or flowering sprigs of thyme.

1.5 kg (3 lb) assorted fresh fruit (apples, apricots, bananas, cherries, figs, guavas, kiwifruit, lychees, nectarines, melons, peaches, oranges, pears, pineapples, plums, strawberries, raspberries, passionfruit, starfruit, blackberries), prepared

---

4—6 tbs Canderel Spoonful

---

300 ml (½ pint) fruit juice or sweet white wine

Borage's bright cobalt-blue flowers look lovely in amongst the fruits and a few mint leaves give added freshness to the macedoine.

Cut the fruits into small cubes or thin slices, as you wish. Put into a large bowl with the Canderel Spoonful to taste and the juice or wine. Mix thoroughly, and chill for several hours before decorating and serving.

PLUMS WITH WATERMELON

SERVES 8—10

Not only are the flavours of this fruit salad exquisite, so also are the colours. A spectacular party piece.

If you wish to serve this compote in the watermelon shell, cut it in half around the circumference in shallow zigzags. Without damaging the shell, remove the ripe pink flesh and

---

1 medium watermelon

---

500 g (1 lb) ripe Victoria plums, stoned and chopped

---

500 g (1 lb) ripe greengages, stoned and chopped

4—6 tbs Canderel Spoonful

---

4 tbs kirsch

---

a few sprigs of fresh mint, to decorate

---

discard the seeds. Cut the fruit into dice, reserving as much juice as possible.

Mix with the prepared plums and greengages, and sweeten to taste with the Canderel Spoonful. Add the reserved juices and the kirsch, and chill thoroughly. Serve decorated with mint leaves, in the watermelon halves, if you wish.

Plums with Watermelon (page 84); Macedoine of Fruits (page 84)

MELON SALAD

SERVES 4–6

This is a dessert with a difference: ground almonds and crème fraîche are mixed in with the fruits, where pale, soft colours are highlighted by the bright-red strawberries used to decorate the dish.

Cut the melon in half and discard the seeds. Scoop out the flesh and chop

1 large, ripe charentais melon
half a ripe pineapple, peeled, and cored
50 g (2 oz) ground almonds
1 tbs lemon juice
4 tbs Canderel Spoonful
125 g (4 oz) crème fraîche or fromage frais
250 g (8 oz) strawberries, hulled and halved, to decorate

it into small dice.

Chop the pineapple and add to the melon. Mix in the ground almonds, lemon juice and Canderel Spoonful. Stir this mixture into the crème fraîche or fromage frais. Chill thoroughly.

Serve decorated with the strawberries.

POIRES À LA BOURGUIGNONNE

SERVES 4

A French classic: pears poached in wine and spices, then served cold. This dish is a splendid and popular finale to a dinner party.

Peel the pears, leaving the stalks and cores in place. Put them into a large bowl of water with the lemon juice so that they do not discolour. Combine the water, wine, spices and peel in a saucepan large enough to

1 kg (2 lb) small pears
juice of half a lemon
150 ml (¼ pint) water
300 ml (½ pint) red burgundy
5 cm (2-inch) stick of cinnamon
1 clove
1 strip orange peel
1 strip lemon peel
5 tbs Canderel Spoonful

contain the pears, and bring to the boil. Add the pears, cover the

saucepan and simmer gently for 15–18 minutes, or until tender. The cooking time will depend on the ripeness of the pears. Cool in the juices. Strain the juices and sweeten with the Canderel Spoonful. Arrange the pears in a serving dish, pour the juices over them, and chill thoroughly, turning from time to time. Serve very cold, with crème fraîche to pass around.

Poires à la Bourguignonne (page 86); Melon Salad (page 86)

CHOCOLATE APPLES
SERVES 4–6

I have been making this simple and delicious dessert for years, for family and friends alike. The grated chocolate is sprinkled over the baked apple slices while they are still hot, so that it hardens to form a crust when the dessert is chilled.

750 g (1½ lb) dessert apples, peeled, cored and sliced
1 tsp ground cloves
4–5 tbs Canderel Spoonful
250 g (8 oz) plain chocolate, grated
Heat the oven to Gas Mark 4/ 180°C/350°F.

Put the apple slices into a baking dish. Mix with a little water and the ground cloves. Cook, covered with foil, in the oven until very soft, about 15 minutes.

Turn into a glass dish. Allow to cool a little, then sweeten to taste with the Canderel Spoonful. Sprinkle a thick layer of grated chocolate over the top. Chill, and serve very cold.

APPLE AND TANGERINE COMPOTE
SERVES 4

This simple compote is light and fresh, an ideal dessert for a family meal. Serve it with Yogurt Dessert Sauce (see page 117), or set yogurt, and some light biscuits.

Grate the tangerine peel. Remove

4 tangerines
300 ml (½ pint) water
350 g (12 oz) apples, peeled, cored and sliced
4–5 tbs Canderel Spoonful

any remaining peel, then divide the fruit into segments. Simmer the grated peel in the water for 5 minutes, then gently poach the sliced apples in it, covered, for 5–6 minutes, until softened.

Allow to cool a little, then sweeten to taste with the Canderel Spoonful. Add the tangerine sections and spoon into a glass dish. Chill.

CHEESECAKES, MOULDS AND SYLLABUBS

BLACKCURRANT CHEESECAKE WITH COTTAGE CHEESE

SERVES 8

The use of cottage cheese and crème fraîche makes this a very delicate, summery cheesecake, which is served with an exquisite blackcurrant sauce.

Purée the cottage cheese in a liquidiser, then beat it with the honey for 2 minutes. Carry on beating as you add the egg yolks one at a time, and beat together thoroughly. Then beat in the orange juice, 1 tablespoon of the lemon juice, vanilla, and crème fraîche. Next beat in the flour. Beat the egg whites until they are frothy, add the cream of tartar and beat again until stiff. Fold gently but thoroughly into the cheese mixture.

Pour the filling into the

500 g (1 lb) cottage cheese
2 tbs clear honey
4 eggs, separated
5 tbs orange juice
2 tbs fresh lemon juice
2 tsp vanilla essence
125 g (4 oz) crème fraîche or fromage frais
3 tbs plain flour
1 tsp cream of tartar
Hot Crumb Crust (see page 124)
1 kg (2 lb) blackcurrants, topped and tailed
1 tsp cornflour
6 tbs Canderel Spoonful
Heat the oven to Gas Mark 8/ 230°C/450°F.

Hot Crumb Crust base and put on to the lowest shelf of the oven. Immediately reduce the heat to Gas Mark 2/150°C/300°F and bake for 50 minutes. Let it cool in the oven with the door ajar for at least 3 hours, then chill overnight. Run a sharp knife that has been dipped in hot water around the inside of the tin, and transfer the cheesecake to a serving dish.

Put 500 g (1 lb) of the blackcurrants into a liquidiser with the remaining lemon juice and the cornflour, and blend to a purée. Put into a small saucepan and cook over a moderate heat, stirring, until it has thickened. Strain into a small bowl, and sweeten with the Canderel Spoonful. Arrange the rest of the blackcurrants over and around the cheesecake, and pour over some of the sauce. Serve the rest separately.

St Clement's Cheesecake (page 93); Blackcurrant Cheesecake with Cottage Cheese (page 90)

FRESH-FRUIT CHEESECAKE
SERVES 8

This smooth orange and lemon cheesecake looks wonderful with its decoration of pale-green kiwifruit, bright-red strawberries and dark-red cherries.

Put the fromage frais, beaten eggs, honey and finely grated peel of the fruit into a liquidiser. Add the fruit juice and the vanilla, and blend. Pour

500 g (1 lb) fromage frais
5 eggs, beaten
4 tbs clear honey, warmed
grated peel and juice of 1 lemon
grated peel and juice of 1 orange
2 tsp vanilla essence
Cold Crumb Crust (see page 125)
500 g (1 lb) mixed black cherries, strawberries and kiwifruit, prepared and sliced
a little Canderel Spoonful
Heat the oven to Gas Mark 2/ 150°C/300°F.

on to the prepared base and bake in the oven for 1 hour. Turn off the heat and leave the cheesecake there for 10 minutes, then cool on a rack. Remove from the tin.

Arrange the sliced fruits over the top of the cheesecake. Sprinkle with a little Canderel Spoonful and serve.

COEURS À LA CRÈME
SERVES 4

One of my favourite things. I first had these little individual heart-shaped delicacies in France years ago, served with a raspberry sauce, and I have never forgotten how good they were. Here is my version of the classic French dessert.

Beat together the fromage frais, Canderel Spoonful and soft cheese

300 g (10 oz) fromage frais
4 tbs Canderel Spoonful
125 g (4 oz) low-fat soft cheese
Melba Sauce (see page 122)
TO DECORATE:
4 whole raspberries
4 sprigs of mint

until smooth. Line four 7.5 cm (3-inch) heart-shaped moulds or biscuit cutters with clean muslin.

Spoon the cheese mixture into the moulds and smooth the tops. Place the moulds around the edge of a plate and leave to drain overnight in the refrigerator.

Invert onto 4 small serving plates. Carefully remove the muslin and pour the Melba Sauce around each heart. Decorate with the raspberries and mint sprigs.

ST CLEMENT'S CHEESECAKE

SERVES 6–8

This is a very 'cheesy' cheesecake, fairly mild in taste but with a good texture – it rises in a spectacular fashion. I like to serve it with one of the fruit sauces on pages 114–122.

Cream the cheese with a fork, and mix in the fromage blanc and the crème fraîche, or cream. Whisk the eggs and egg yolks together with the honey, orange and lemon juices and peel, the vanilla and the flour. Add to

150 g (5 oz) low-fat soft cheese
750 g (1½ lb) fromage blanc
125 g (4 oz) crème fraîche or double or whipping cream, whipped
2 eggs
2 egg yolks
3 tbs clear honey
grated peel and juice of 1 orange
grated peel and juice of 1 lemon
2 tsp vanilla essence
3 oz plain flour
2 tbs kirsch (optional)
Heat the oven to Gas Mark 5/ 190°C/375°F.

the cream-cheese mixture. Flavour if desired with the kirsch.

Pour on to the prepared base and bake in the bottom of the oven for 1 hour. Cool in the oven with the door ajar for 25 minutes, to prevent it from collapsing, then cool on a rack for 2–3 hours.

Run a sharp knife around the inside of the tin to loosen the cheesecake, and turn it out.

RICE TYROLHOF

SERVES 4

With its lovely rum flavour this rice mould is an excellent pudding for cold weather, served with a cold fruit sauce of your choice (see pages 114–122).

Cook the rice in the milk until it is tender and all the liquid is absorbed, about 30–35 minutes, stirring frequently to prevent the rice sticking to the base of the pan. Leave

5 tbs long-grain rice
15 g (½ oz) gelatine
juice of 1 orange
600 ml (1 pint) skimmed milk
6 tbs Canderel Spoonful
1 dessert apple, peeled, cored and diced finely
75 g (3 oz) seedless grapes, peeled and halved
2 tbs rum
2 tbs crème fraîche or fromage frais
1 egg white

to cool. Soak the gelatine in the orange juice. Add the Canderel Spoonful to the rice, then add the gelatine. Add the apple and the grapes. Fold in first the crème fraîche and the rum, and then beat the egg white until stiff and fold in.

Pour the mixture into a lightly oiled charlotte mould, and chill. When set, turn out on to a serving dish.

Rice Tyrolhof (page 93); Tipsy Syllabub (page 96); Coeurs à la Crème (page 92)

TIPSY SYLLABUB

SERVES 4

Syllabubs made either with Greek yogurt or with crème fraîche are a revelation in taste; they are fresh, light and still creamy but not heavy on the stomach. This one, made with Grand Marnier and strawberries, is pure delight.

grated peel and juice of 1 orange
4 tbs Grand Marnier
4–6 tbs Canderel Spoonful
500 g (1 lb) Greek yogurt
½ tsp grated nutmeg
250 g (8 oz) strawberries, hulled and sliced

Mix the orange peel and juice with the Grand Marnier and leave overnight. Strain into a large bowl and sweeten with the Canderel Spoonful. Stir in the Greek yogurt slowly, then add the grated nutmeg. Beat thoroughly.

Put the strawberries into the bottom of 4 individual glasses, and spoon the syllabub mixture over them. Chill overnight, until set.

FRUIT TERRINE

SERVES 6—8

This elegant-looking dessert is basically a layered fruit jelly. It takes time and patience but is exquisitely pretty with all the different fruit colours surrounded by a pale, translucent jelly. Worthy of a special family occasion.

15 g (½ oz) gelatine
3 tbs hot water
450 ml (¾ pint) apple juice
3 tbs Canderel Spoonful
750 g (1½ lb) assorted fresh fruit (oranges, bananas, strawberries, seedless grapes, dessert apples, peaches), prepared and sliced

Dissolve the gelatine in the hot water. Rinse a 750 g (1½ lb) loaf tin with cold water. Mix the apple juice with the dissolved gelatine and the Canderel Spoonful. Pour a thin layer into the tin and leave to set in the fridge. Keep the rest of the mixture warm. When the first layer has set, make a pretty pattern on top with two of the fruits, say grapes and bananas, and cover with more of the jelly mixture. Leave to set again. Continue making layers in this way with the various fruits, making sure that the last layer of fruit is completely covered with apple jelly. Leave to set overnight in the fridge.

To serve, dip the tin quickly into hot water and invert on to a serving plate. Cut into thin slices with a sharp knife. Serve with Greek yogurt or Crème Chantilly (see page 116).

ORANGE SYLLABUB

SERVES 4

This is a classic syllabub, fruity and smooth yet light and delicate. A perfect dessert for a summer party.

Mix the orange peel and juice with the wine, and leave for several hours. Strain into a bowl and add the

grated peel and juice of 1 orange
6 tbs medium white wine
4–5 tbs Canderel Spoonful
350 g (12 oz) crème fraîche or double or whipping cream, whipped

Canderel Spoonful. Stir until dissolved, then beat in the crème fraîche or cream slowly, so that the mixture amalgamates.

Whisk thoroughly, then spoon into individual glasses and leave overnight to set.

LEMON YOGURT SYLLABUB

SERVES 4

This wonderfully fresh syllabub is made with yogurt and skimmed-milk powder to give it an extra lightness, while the chopped walnuts add a slight crunchiness.

Mix the yogurt with the dried milk, Canderel Spoonful, lemon peel and juice, and whisk well. Chill for

500 g (1 lb) low-fat natural yogurt
6 tbs skimmed-milk powder
4–6 tbs Canderel Spoonful
grated peel of 2 lemons
4 tbs fresh lemon juice
50 g (2 oz) walnut pieces, chopped finely
1 egg white
4 strips of lemon peel, to decorate

45 minutes, or until beginning to thicken.

Fold in the chopped walnuts, then beat the egg white until stiff and fold in. Spoon into individual glasses, and leave to set for 2–3 hours.

Decorate each syllabub with a curl of lemon peel.

ALMOND RUSSE

SERVES 6—8

A delectably sophisticated dessert, sweet, rich and nutty, this is dinner-party material. It was invented by the great nineteenth-century chef, Carème, and survives to this day in different forms. Here is a light version designed to suit modern tastes.

Cream the margarine with 6 tablespoons of the Canderel Spoonful and stir in the almond essence and the brandy. Beat in the

175 g (6 oz) sunflower margarine, plus a little extra for greasing
8 tbs Canderel Spoonful
½ tsp almond essence
1 tbs brandy
3 eggs, separated
125 g (4 oz) ground almonds
125 g (4 oz) almonds, toasted
350 g (12 oz) crème fraîche
12 lady's fingers
6 almonds

egg yolks, then add the ground

almonds and beat again. Stir in the toasted almonds, then fold in the crème fraîche.

Beat the egg whites until frothy, add the rest of the Canderel Spoonful and beat again to very stiff peaks. Fold into the almond mixture.

Line a greased trifle dish with the lady's fingers, pour in the mixture and chill for 24 hours. Invert on to a serving plate and decorate with the whole almonds.

Almond Russe (page 98); Crème Beau Rivage (page 102)

BLACKBERRY SYLLABUB

SERVES 4

This autumn speciality is based on an old English recipe from the days when people treated a syllabub as a drink rather than as a dessert. So it is thinner than the syllabub we are used to – but none the less delicious.

---
500 g (1 lb) ripe blackberries, hulled

---
juice of half a lemon

---
2 tbs water

3–4 tbs Canderel Spoonful

---
250 g (8 oz) crème fraîche or double or whipping cream, whipped

---

Put the blackberries into a saucepan with the lemon juice and water and stew gently, covered for 10 minutes. Leave to cool in the juices. Strain when cold, reserving the juices, then sweeten the fruit with the Canderel Spoonful.

Measure off 300 ml (½ pint) of the juices into a bowl and sweeten with a little Canderel Spoonful. Gradually beat in the crème fraîche or cream, whisking well.

Chill for 2–3 hours, then serve in tall drinking glasses.

RASPBERRY CHEESE SYLLABUB

SERVES 4

This syllabub has a slightly grainy texture which complements the raspberries which lie at the bottom. It is easily made and is lovely as part of a simple summer's meal.

---
250 g (8 oz) cottage cheese

---
4 tbs Canderel Spoonful

---
finely grated peel of 1 orange

---
3 tbs sweet white wine

---
175 g (6 oz) Greek or set yogurt

---
250 g (8 oz) raspberries, hulled

---
twists of orange peel, to decorate

Put the cottage cheese into a liquidiser with the Canderel Spoonful, orange peel and white wine, and blend until smooth. Pass through a fine sieve, then blend in the yogurt.

Put the raspberries into the bottom of 4 individual glasses, and spoon the syllabub over the top. Chill for at least 4 hours. Serve decorated with a twist of orange peel over the edge of each glass.

Orange Syllabub (page 97); Blackberry Syllabub (page 100); Raspberry Cheese Syllabub (page 100)

CRÈME BEAU RIVAGE

SERVES 4

This very light mould is delicately flavoured with tangerines and orange liqueur. Serve it with Peach Sauce (see page 116) as the delectable finale to a dinner party.

Soak the gelatine in the water. Finely grate the peel of the tangerines and add it to the warmed milk. Heat gently for 2 minutes, then pour over the egg yolks, stirring constantly. Beat in the cornflour. Return to the pan and cook gently, stirring all the time, until it thickens.

15 g (½ oz) gelatine
3 tbs water
3 tangerines
150 ml (¼ pint) skimmed milk, warmed
3 egg yolks
1 tsp cornflour
3 tbs Canderel Spoonful
2 tbs Grand Marnier
250 g (8 oz) crème fraîche or fromage frais, mashed
2 egg whites

Strain and cool, then stir in the Canderel Spoonful.

Heat the gelatine gently in a small saucepan until it is runny, and add to the custard. Chill for 15 minutes.

Peel the tangerines and divide them into segments. Fold the segments into the crème fraîche or fromage frais, then fold this into the custard and stir in the Grand Marnier. Next, beat the egg whites until stiff and fold in. Turn into a soufflé mould and chill until fully set, about 6 hours.

STUFFED FRUIT
DESSERTS

STUFFED MELON

SERVES 4

Fresh and fruity, this recipe for chilled stuffed melon is simple, but effective.

Score the flesh of the melon without damaging the skin, marking it into cubes so that it will lift away easily with a spoon. Sprinkle with lemon juice and chill.

Mix the crème fraîche or

1 honeydew melon, halved and de-seeded
1 tbs lemon juice
350 g (12 oz) crème fraîche or fromage frais
4 tbs Canderel Spoonful
2 bananas, peeled and diced
250 g (8 oz) seedless grapes, halved
2 egg whites
mint sprigs, to decorate

fromage frais with half of the Canderel Spoonful and stir in the prepared fruits. Beat the egg whites until stiff then fold in the Canderel Spoonful. Beat again until very stiff, and fold into the crème fraîche or fromage frais mixture. Fill the melon halves with the mixture and chill thoroughly. Serve decorated with mint sprigs.

STUFFED PLUMS SABAYON

SERVES 4

This dish of stuffed plums, in puff pastry and deep-fried in light oil, is unforgettable.

Put the plums in a bowl, cover with boiling water, and leave for 2 minutes. Slip off the skins under cold water. Cut the plums carefully down the middle, but not all the way through, and remove the stones. Mix the ground almonds with the macaroons and add enough egg white to bind to a very stiff paste.

8 ripe Victoria plums, peeled
50 g (2 oz) ground almonds
50 g (2 oz) macaroons, crumbled
1 egg white
175 g (6 oz) frozen puff pastry, thawed
Sauce Sabayon (see page 122)

Fill the plum cavities with this mixture.

Roll out the puff pastry thinly and cut into circles big enough to wrap the plums in. Dampen the

edges with a little water, and press together securely.

To deep-fry them, heat some vegetable oil to 190°C/375°F (or until a cube of day-old bread browns in 10–15 seconds). Put the plums in the oil and deep-fry, turning, until golden brown all over, about 1 minute. Drain on kitchen paper.

To serve, place two stuffed plums per person into individual glass dishes, and pour the Sauce Sabayon over the top.

Stuffed Melon (page 104); Stuffed Plums Sabayon (page 104)

Deep-fried Stuffed Apricots (page 109); Pears Milanese (page 108); Apples Stuffed with Blackberries (page 109); Stuffed Baked

Peaches (page 108)

STUFFED BAKED PEACHES
SERVES 6

This stunning dish of ripe peaches, stuffed with macaroon crumbs, almonds and glacé fruits, is summer party food par excellence. Lovely served with crème fraîche, and any leftovers are delicious cold.

Marinate the peaches in the wine overnight. Heat the oven to Gas Mark 4/180°C/350°F. Combine the

6 ripe peaches, peeled, halved and stoned
150 ml (¼ pint) white wine
1 tbs chopped mixed glacé fruits
75 g (3 oz) macaroons, crushed
50 g (2 oz) slivered almonds, toasted
2 tbs clear honey, warmed
a little Canderel Spoonful

glacé fruits, macaroons and almonds with the honey, and fill the peach cavities with the mixture.

Put the filled peaches into a large baking dish and pour the wine juices over the top. Bake in the oven for 20 minutes. Sprinkle with a little Canderel Spoonful just before serving.

PEARS MILANESE
SERVES 6

This recipe from northern Italy demonstrates the affinity between pears and hazelnuts – the delicate flavour of the fruit is enhanced by the aromatic nuts. Delicious served with Crème Chantilly (see page 116).

Cut the pears in half lengthways and scoop out the cores. Mix the chopped

6 large firm pears
50 g (2 oz) glacé cherries, chopped finely
125 g (4 oz) hazelnuts, toasted and ground coarsely
2 tbs clear honey, warmed
¼ tsp almond essence
125 ml (4 fl oz) dry sherry
Heat the oven to Gas Mark 4/ 180°C/350°F.

honey and almond essence, and fill the pear halves with this mixture. Place in a well-greased baking dish and trickle the sherry over the top.

Bake in the oven for 15 minutes, basting with the juices from time to time, until tender but not mushy.

Serve hot or warm, with Crème Chantilly.

cherries with the ground hazelnuts,

D E E P - F R I E D   S T U F F E D
A P R I C O T S
S E R V E S   4—6

Mouthwatering morsels, these apricots are stuffed with dates and nuts, and coated in fine breadcrumbs before being deep-fried briefly in light oil. You can also use nectarines.

Immerse the apricots or nectarines in boiling water for 1 minute, then peel them with a sharp knife. Cut a slit down the side of each fruit and carefully remove the stone without

12 ripe apricots or nectarines
12 almonds, toasted
12 dates, stoned
2 tsp lemon juice
1 egg, beaten
1 tbs melted butter, cooled
125 g (4 oz) fine wholemeal breadcrumbs

damaging the flesh. Put a toasted almond into each date, place in the fruit cavity, and close it up.

Combine the beaten egg with the cooled melted butter in a small bowl, and dip the apricots in the mixture. Roll them in the breadcrumbs and deep-fry in vegetable oil heated to 190°C/375°F until golden brown.

Lift out with a slotted spoon, drain on kitchen paper, and serve as soon as possible, with a bowl of Yogurt Dessert Sauce (see page 117) for dipping.

A P P L E S   S T U F F E D
W I T H   B L A C K B E R R I E S
S E R V E S   4

It is surprising how delicious the simple device of filling apples with blackberries, and baking them, can be. This is an autumnal treat in which we often indulge at home, using windfalls from the Bramley apple tree that stands on the lawn.

Slit the apple skin round the middle

4 large apples, (preferably Bramleys) cored
250 g (8 oz) ripe blackberries, hulled
2 tbs clear honey
40 g (1½ oz) sunflower margarine
Crème Chantilly (see page 116)
Heat the oven to Gas Mark 4/ 180°C/350°F.

then hollow out the cavities a little,

and fill each one with a quarter of the blackberries. Trickle a little honey over the blackberries and dot with the margarine.

Bake for 20 minutes in the oven, until soft but not mushy. Serve hot or warm, with the Crème Chantilly.

STUFFED PEARS IN APRICOT SAUCE
SERVES 6

This is a marvellous dessert for a dinner party, with its melting textures and delicate flavours. The soft stuffing, made with ground almonds and finely grated chocolate, complements the fine flavour of the pears to perfection.

Peel the pears carefully, leaving the stalks in place. Remove the cores, starting from the base of the fruit, using a sharp knife and without piercing through the top of the fruit.

6 firm, ripe pears
4 tbs fresh lemon juice
50 g (2 oz) trifle sponge crumbs
25 g (1 oz) ground almonds
25 (1 oz) plain chocolate, grated finely
40 g (1½ oz) sunflower margarine, melted
1 tbs Canderel Spoonful
Apricot Sauce (see page 116)
Heat the oven to Gas Mark 3/ 160°C/325°F.

Brush the pears with the lemon juice. Stand in a well-buttered baking dish with a little water, cover with foil, and bake in the oven for 15 minutes, until tender but still firm. Leave for a while to cool.

Mix together the sponge crumbs, ground almonds and grated chocolate, and stir in the melted sunflower margarine and the Canderel Spoonful. Fill the centre of each pear with this mixture. Slice the pears and arrange in a shallow serving dish. Coat with the Apricot Sauce and serve with crème fraîche.

SCHEHERAZADE'S MELON
SERVES 4–6

This doesn't quite have a thousand and one different fruits in it, but it is an exotic mixture of fine fruits with champagne and kirsch. It's a wonderful dessert for a summer party.

Cut the top off the melon, about 7.5 cm (3-inches) down from the stem end, and reserve the lid. Cut a thin slice off the other end so that the fruit can stand upright. Scoop out the seeds, then carefully remove all

1 large honeydew melon
1 ripe peach, peeled, stoned and diced
2 slices pineapple, diced
1 ripe banana, sliced thinly
125 g (4 oz) strawberries, hulled
125 g (4 oz) raspberries, hulled
125 ml (4 fl oz) champagne
3 tbs kirsch
3–4 tbs Canderel Spoonful
sprigs of fresh herbs, to decorate

the flesh, without damaging the skin. Reserve as much juice as possible.

Dice the fruit, and mix with all the other prepared fruits. Add the melon juices, the champagne and the kirsch. Sweeten to taste with the Canderel Spoonful, then put all the fruit back into the melon skin and stand it on a plate. Chill for several hours. Serve with the lid replaced on the top and a garland of herbs around the melon.

Stuffed Pears in Apricot Sauce (page 110)

BAKED PEARS WITH CHEESE

SERVES 4

Half-sweet, half-savoury, this unusual dessert is gorgeous on a chilly winter's evening.

Peel the pears, leaving the stalks in place. Cut in half and scoop out the core, enlarging the cavity a little. Mash the two cheeses together and spoon the mixture into the pear

4 ripe pears
75 g (3 oz) Stilton
75 g (3 oz) low-fat soft cheese
1 tsp ground cinnamon
a little Canderel Spoonful
Heat the oven to Gas Mark 4/ 180°C/350°F.

cavities. Sandwich them together again and place in a well-greased baking dish with a little water. Sprinkle with cinnamon and cover with foil.

Cook in the oven for 15–20 minutes, or until soft; the cooking time will depend on the ripeness of the pears.

Serve warm, sprinkled with a little Canderel Spoonful.

Baked Pears with Cheese (page 112)

DESSERT SAUCES

CRÈME PATISSIÈRE
MAKES 350 ML (12 FL OZ)

2 egg yolks
1 tbs clear honey
3 tbs plain flour
300 ml (½ pint) skimmed milk, warmed
2 tsp vanilla essence
3–4 tbs Canderel Spoonful

Beat the egg yolks with the honey until pale. Stir in the flour and beat with a whisk until smooth. Add the warmed milk gradually, whisking all the time, then return to the saucepan. Simmer over a very gentle heat, stirring constantly, until the mixture is thick. Leave to cool, then add the vanilla and the Canderel Spoonful. Use as required.

ORANGE SAUCE
MAKES 300 ML (½ PINT)

75 g (3 oz) fromage blanc
2 tbs finely grated orange peel
1 tbs plain flour
1 egg, separated
125 ml (4 fl oz) orange juice
1 tbs lemon juice
4 tbs Canderel Spoonful
125 g (4 oz) crème fraîche or Greek yogurt

Stir the fromage blanc, then mix in the orange peel and flour. Mix in the egg yolk (keeping the egg white for another dish) and stir in the orange juice. Place in a bowl over a pan of hot water and whisk until the sauce thickens. Leave to cool, then add the lemon juice, the Canderel Spoonful and the crème fraîche or Greek yogurt.

LEMON SAUCE
SERVES 3–4

150 ml (¼ pint) natural set yogurt
125 g (4 oz) crème fraîche or fromage frais
4 tbs lemon juice
4 tbs Canderel Spoonful

Mix all the ingredients together until smooth. Chill.

APRICOT SAUCE

MAKES 450 ML (¾ PINT)

Put the apricots into a liquidiser with the lemon juice and the Crème Anglaise and blend to a smooth

250 g (8 oz) ripe apricots, peeled, stoned and sliced

2 tsp lemon juice

300 ml (½ pint) Crème Anglaise, (see page 120)

a little Canderel Spoonful

sauce. Sweeten to taste with Canderel Spoonful. Serve warm or cold.

PEACH SAUCE

MAKES 300 ML (½ PINT)

Put the peaches in a bowl and soak them in boiling water for 2 minutes. Peel, stone and slice them. Put into a liquidiser with the crème fraîche or

2 large ripe peaches

250 g (8 oz) crème fraîche or Greek yogurt

2 tbs Canderel Spoonful

Greek yogurt and blend to a smooth sauce. Sweeten with the Canderel Spoonful.

CRÈME CHANTILLY

SERVES 4–6

Mix the crème fraîche or cream with the Canderel Spoonful, and flavour with the vanilla essence. Beat the

250 g (8 oz) crème fraîche or double or whipping cream, whipped

2 tbs Canderel Spoonful

2 tsp vanilla essence

1 egg white

egg white until stiff then fold it in quickly but thoroughly, and chill. Use the same day you make it.

YOGURT DESSERT SAUCE

SERVES 4

125 g (4 oz) fromage blanc
2 tbs natural set yogurt
1 tsp vanilla essence
2 tbs Canderel Spoonful

Mix the fromage blanc with the set yogurt and add the vanilla. Stir in the Canderel Spoonful, check for sweetness and add more if necessary. Chill.

This sauce is a healthier substitute for double cream, and you can use it as such to accompany the dessert of your choice. It also makes an excellent topping, or a filling for cakes. To make a thinner, special sauce you can flavour the mixture with the grated peel of lemon or orange, and kirsch, brandy or cassis.

TROPICAL-FRUIT SAUCE

SERVES 4

125 g (4 oz) cottage cheese
125 g (4 oz) natural yogurt
5 tbs tropical-fruit juice
grated peel of 1 orange
3 tbs Canderel Spoonful

Put all the ingredients into a liquidiser and blend thoroughly. Chill.

HOT BLACKCURRANT SAUCE

MAKES 300 ML (½ PINT)

350 g (12 oz) blackcurrants, topped and tailed
1 tbs cornflour
2–3 tablespoons Canderel Spoonful
1 tsp grated lemon peel
2 tsp cassis syrup (optional)

Blend the blackcurrants thoroughly in a liquidizer. Sieve to remove the pips. Heat gently in a small saucepan, then stir a little into the cornflour. Add the rest, stirring all the time, then bring to the boil. Cool a little, then add the Canderel Spoonful. Add the lemon peel and cassis syrup, if desired, then serve.

Apricot Sauce (page 116); Orange Sauce (page 115); Peach Sauce (page 116); Lemon Sauce (page 115); Crème Patissière (page 115) (in preparation)

CRÈME ANGLAISE

MAKES 350 ML (12 FL OZ)

2 egg yolks
2 tbs clear honey
1 tbs cornflour
300 ml (½ pint) skimmed milk, heated
2 tsp vanilla essence
3 tbs Canderel Spoonful
125 g (4 oz) crème fraîche or double or whipping cream, whipped (optional)

Beat the egg yolks with the honey until pale and light, and stir in the cornflour. Pour the hot milk over this mixture, stirring, and return it to the saucepan. Cook very gently over a low heat, stirring constantly. Turn the heat right down and let it simmer for 5 minutes in order to cook the cornflour. Leave to cool a little, stir in the vanilla essence, then add the Canderel Spoonful.

For a richer custard, beat the crème fraîche or cream into the cooled Crème Anglaise just before serving.

This keeps for 2 days in the fridge.

CHOCOLATE SAUCE

MAKES 450 ML (¾ PINT)

75 g (3 oz) plain chocolate
300 ml (½ pint) water
1 tsp cocoa powder
1 tsp instant coffee powder
2 tsp vanilla essence
3 tbs Canderel Spoonful

Dissolve the chocolate in the water over a low heat, stirring constantly, then add the cocoa and instant coffee and simmer until the sauce thickens, about 5 minutes. Cool, then add the vanilla essence and sweeten with the Canderel Spoonful.

Crème Anglaise (page 120) (in preparation); Chocolate Sauce (page 120) (in preparation)

SAUCE SABAYON

MAKES 300 ML (½ PINT)

Beat the egg yolks with the honey until thick, and stir in the cornflour. Add the wine or juice and the lemon peel and beat thoroughly. Place in a

3 egg yolks
2 tbs clear honey
1 tbs cornflour
1 wineglass sweet white wine or fruit juice
1 tsp grated lemon peel
2–3 tbs Canderel Spoonful

bowl over a pan of hot water and whisk until thick. Cool a little, then sweeten to taste with the Canderel Spoonful.

LIGHT CHOCOLATE SAUCE

MAKES 450 ML (¾ PINT)

Mix the water into the cocoa and simmer gently, stirring until smooth, for 10 minutes. Cool, and add the

300 ml (½ pint) boiling water
50 g (2 oz) cocoa powder
1 tsp vanilla essence
6–8 tbs Canderel Spoonful

vanilla essence and the Canderel Spoonful.

SIMPLE FRUIT SAUCE

SERVES 4

Moisten the cornflour with a little of the fruit juice and stir until smooth. Slowly add the rest of the juice. Heat gently in a small saucepan, stirring

1 tbs cornflour
300 ml (½ pint) fruit juice of your choice
2 tbs Canderel Spoonful

all the time, until the mixture thickens. Cool, then add the Canderel Spoonful. Serve warm or cold.

MELBA SAUCE

MAKES 450 ML (¾ PINT)

Blend the prepared raspberries thoroughly in a liquidiser. Sieve to remove the pips, and sweeten the

500 g (1 lb) raspberries, hulled
3–4 tbs Canderel Spoonful

pulp with the Canderel Spoonful. Leave to chill.

BASIC RECIPES

SWEET CRUST PASTRY

Crumble the margarine into the flour until it resembles fine breadcrumbs. Mix in the warmed honey and knead to a light pastry on a floured board. Cover, and chill for at least 1 hour. Roll out on a floured board when ready to use.

TO LINE A 20 CM (8-INCH) FLAN TIN:

75 g (3 oz) sunflower margarine

175 g (6 oz) plain flour, sifted

2 tbs clear honey, warmed

Heat the oven to Gas Mark 3/ 160°C/325°F.

TO BAKE BLIND

Line a well-buttered 20 cm (8-inch) flan tin with the rolled out pastry and trim the edges. Prick the pastry with a fork. Line it with a sheet of foil and fill with dried beans. Bake for 10–15 minutes, then remove the foil and beans and return the pastry to the oven for a further 5 minutes until crisp and lightly browned.

HOT CRUMB CRUST

Melt the margarine with the honey and stir into the crumbs. Mix very thoroughly, and press into the base of a loose-bottomed cake tin, or use

---
TO LINE A 20 CM (8-INCH) FLAN TIN:

75 g (3 oz) sunflower margarine

2 tbs clear honey

250 g (8 oz) digestive-biscuit crumbs

Heat the oven to Gas Mark 4/ 180°C/350°F.

---

it to line a flan case. Bake in the oven for 10 minutes, and allow to cool before putting in the filling.

BASIC CRÊPES
MAKES 12

Put all the ingredients into a liquidiser and blend thoroughly. Leave to stand for at least 2 hours before using.

Grease an 18 cm (7-inch) frying pan. Heat, then pour in one-twelfth of the batter, tipping the pan

150 g (5 oz) plain flour, sifted
2 large eggs
300 ml (½ pint) skimmed milk
150 ml (¼ pint) water
15 g (½ oz) sunflower margarine, melted
1 tbs clear honey, warmed

so that the batter covers it. Cook until golden underneath. Turn and cook the other side.

Slide the crêpe on to a plate and repeat until the rest of the batter is used up.

COLD CRUMB CRUST

Mix the melted margarine into the crumbs thoroughly, and stir in the Canderel Spoonful. Press into a

TO LINE A 20 CM (8-INCH) FLAN TIN:
75 g (3 oz) sunflower margarine, melted
250 g (8 oz) digestive-biscuit crumbs
4 tbs Canderel Spoonful

loose-bottomed cake tin or flan case, and chill.

BASIC SOUFFLÉ-OMELETTE
SERVES 4

Soufflé-omelettes make brilliant puddings – they look spectacular and intricate, yet they are easier to prepare than almost any other party dessert. The timing of course is crucial – it is only a matter of minutes from oven to table.

Beat the egg yolks with the honey and cornflour until the mixture is

3 eggs, separated
3 tbs clear honey
1 tsp cornflour
Heat the oven to Gas Mark 7/ 220°C/425°F.

light and creamy. Beat the egg whites to form stiff peaks. Fold quickly and smoothly into the yolk mixture.

Lightly grease a large heavy-bottomed pan, and put half of the egg mixture into it, smoothing it down to a round shape. Brown the omelette lightly on one side. Put any filling over half of the top, fold over, and put into the oven for 3 minutes, or until the middle of the omelette is lightly set but still moist. Make the second omelette in the same way.

Basic Crêpes (page 125) (in preparation)